SOUL
COMMUNICATION

SOUL
COMMUNICATION

CONNECT WITH YOUR BILLION DOLLAR INNER-GUIDE AND UNCOVER YOUR MOST AUTHENTIC SELF.

OLIVIA BLAKEY

SOUL COMMUNICATION
CONNECT WITH YOUR BILLION DOLLAR INNER-GUIDE
AND UNCOVER YOUR MOST AUTHENTIC SELF.

iUniverse books may be ordered through booksellers or by contacting:

iUniverse
1663 Liberty Drive
Bloomington, IN 47403
www.iuniverse.com
844-349-9409

ISBN: 978-1-6632-0964-1 (sc)
ISBN: 978-1-6632-0966-5 (hc)
ISBN: 978-1-6632-0965-8 (e)

Print information available on the last page.

iUniverse rev. date: 06/30/2021

CONTENTS

ACKNOWLEDGEMENTS

"Because we live in a world of oneness, where unity is a superpower."

For my family – thank you for supporting me in everything I do.
For my soulmate – thank you for your dedication to unconditional love.
For every horse I have ridden through time and space –
thank you for reminding me to live from the heart.
For all music producers – thank you for creating a universal language.
For every writer – thank you for inspiring me to share my story.
For my proof-readers – thank you for dedicating
your time to Soul Communication.
For the divine masculine – thank you for protecting the divine feminine.
For the divine feminine – thank you for healing the divine masculine.
For astrology – thank you for being a beautiful
metaphor for rebirth and transformation.
For the mind, body and soul – thank you for being a powerful team.
For my ancestors – thank you for paving the way.
For my future children – thank you for continuing this legacy.
And for you – thank you for purchasing this book
and being committed to soulful evolution.

SYNOPSIS

*"I choose to consciously move from fear to
love, transcending darkness to light."*

Designed to help sensitive souls intentionally align with the callings of their higher self, Soul Communication is a guide to manifesting soul alignment and becoming the creator of one's own unique path of abundance.

Shaped by a story of the cyclic nature of death and rebirth through an astrological metaphor, the journey includes twelve powerful exercises of intentional soul work, utilised for transcending darkness to light and fear to love, in all areas of life.

Western medicine calls it 'mental illness.' Ancient shamanic traditions call it 'spiritual emergence.' I call it 'rebirth.'

Rebirth does not have to be painful, but rather, enables you to release old patterns and programming that no longer serve your highest good, so that you can receive the new.

Rebirth does not have to create suffering, but rather, empowers you to heal and free yourself from limiting belief systems that hold you back from living your greatest life.

Rebirth does not have to cause resistance, but rather, awakens you to the beauty and liberation of limitless possibility.

Rebirthing the soul is a natural process of evolution that is often mistaken as a problem or brokenness. Soul Communication transcends this stigma. It reflects the exact reason why humanity must surrender to the cyclic process of change and transformation.

When you align with the language and the blueprint of your soul, you become the creator of your own life.

INTRODUCTION

"Everything in my life is always working out for me because I firmly take action to manifest the things that matter on my life path. The universe always responds to my vibration since the cosmos supports my choices."

This book is an informative approach to rebirthing the soul through combining a variety of mindfulness and intentional writing exercises. This includes journal prompting and invocations. There are twelve Soul Communication exercises to complete, so that you can take yourself on a journey through all dimensions within your life. The aim is to attain balance and wholeness within the elements of mind, body and soul.

The Twelve Soul Communications

- ❖ The 1st Soul Communication – becoming familiar and comfortable with your cyclic nature and the power of transformation.
- ❖ The 2nd Soul Communication – gratitude for your physical reality in the 3rd dimension on planet earth.
- ❖ The 3rd Soul Communication – aligning with your higher mind through transforming the darkest shadows into the brightest light.
- ❖ The 4th Soul Communication – tapping into the positive elements of your divine feminine nature by journeying through the feminine dimension.
- ❖ The 5th Soul Communication – embracing your heart's calling through soulful play, dance, art, and creativity.
- ❖ The 6th Soul Communication – discovering your healing capabilities, being of service to yourself and embodying self-love in all areas of life.
- ❖ The 7th Soul Communication – creating the most beautiful relationships with your soul family and aligning with your most authentic tribe.

❖ The 8ᵗʰ Soul Communication – transforming your fears through surrendering to the process of rebirthing the soul.

❖ The 9ᵗʰ Soul Communication – establishing life, joy, love, and abundance after loss through soul renewal.

❖ The 10ᵗʰ Soul Communication – tapping into the positive elements of your divine masculine nature by journeying through the masculine dimension.

❖ The 11ᵗʰ Soul Communication – aligning with the mission and blueprint of your soul through tapping into frequencies of pure love.

❖ The 12ᵗʰ Soul Communication – appreciation for your spiritual reality in the 5ᵗʰ dimension and intentionally manifesting spirit into matter.

The intention of these exercises is to assist you in stepping into your authenticity. You can achieve this by manifesting the most profound alignment of your soul's mission. When you take action to transcend fear to love, you open doors to unlimited abundance.

In the process of removing all blocks of fear and limiting belief systems, you can become united with 5-dimensional consciousness, which vibrates in a state of pure love, at the highest of frequencies. That is where the magic happens. That is where all judgements of yourself and others are dropped. That is the place where you become the creator of your most unique and authentic life path. That is where you attain all joy and abundance through the process of rebirth.

If there is one thing that is required to soulfully evolve, it is surrender. So, let us begin the journey through the 1ˢᵗ house of Aries, where the birthing of the soul's most authentic identity commences.

CHAPTER 1

THE RAM

"I am connected to the divinity of my soul's identity."

Sign: Aries
Ruler: Mars
Element: Fire
Season: Spring
Colour: Red
Stone: Bloodstone
Light elements: Dynamic, Brave, Bold, Vibrant, Leadership
Shadow elements: Aggressive, Controlling, Combative, Co-dependent

The 1st house that the soul journeys through is Aries, the ram. This house speaks of one's sense of self and how one identifies with themselves in this lifetime. Since rebirthing the soul is an ever-evolving process, we visit the dimension of Aries many times. We always return to this place to realise that we are not just one identity, but rather, we are shaped by multidimensionality within a limitless universe.

This is a place that is symbolic for all newness that enters one's life. Aries reflects that there are forever new beginnings nevertheless waiting for us. Aries is a place of joy, richness, rejuvenation, liveliness, introductions, and inventiveness. Aries is what births heart-based leaders and entrepreneurs into the world. It is the beginning of all manifestation and it is where we can always return to reshape our soul's identity.

We must sculpt our identities with love and authenticity if we are to stand in the light – the positive elements of the house of Aries. When we travel through the opening house, we must remember the power of cyclic nature and the power of transformation. It is here that we develop all parts of the soul, creating the foundational pillars for our career, relationships, lifestyle, and everything else that happens in life.

The truth is born here in the 1ˢᵗ house. We must rise to become the leader of the things we believe are most important in the world. Not only do we develop the identity of our soul, but we also take everything we have learned here and carry it through the entire cycle of astrological houses.

It is Aries that awakens us to our soul's mission and how we must show up in the world. It is Aries that starts the first part of our journey and story, leading the way with our soul's identity throughout the remaining astrological signs. It is Aries that reminds us of our genuine individuality and how we are all living subjective lives.

If anything, this is the most significant sign within the cycle because everything will always come back to who we are and the mission of the soul. Everything will always return to the house of Aries, asking us to apply all matters we have learned throughout life to the evolution of the soul. When you return to Aries after completing the full circuit, this is a beautiful reminder that it is not the end, but rather, it is the beginning of a new adventure in reshaping your mind, body and soul – reconstructing your entire life.

So much rebirthing happens within the house of Aries, for this is the place where we will always return to ourselves, redesigning who we are, what we believe matters most in life and how we can transmute all pain and suffering into the brightest of light.

This place of rebirth is a gift of newness and delightful experience, just like when parents meet their new-born for the first time. We must honour the house of Aries – the symbolism of the ram – because, without the ram's energy, we would not be able to journey through the cyclic process of transformation and the ever-evolving process of rebirth. We would not be able to remember our divinity and the notion of being limitless, eternal souls.

While Aries lights up areas of the ability to be dynamic, brave, bold, vibrant, and lead the way, it also significantly represents the shadow elements that can be aggressive, controlling, combative and co-dependent. We must transcend these shadows into light, moving from a state of fear to love. We must surpass and elevate higher if we are to be the best version of our own identities, releasing all that no longer serves ourselves, others, and the planet.

Being aggressive does not serve anyone. Being controlling, combative, and co-dependent does not help anyone either. These shadow elements can sometimes make souls feel stuck and stagnant in life, which is often due to holding onto the past because of fear of 'endings'. But we must let go of this idea because without endings there are no new beginnings.

If someone is living in these shadow states of being, it is because they are most likely carrying limiting belief systems shaped around fear and separation. These shadow elements must be transformed to reflect the very opposite. The truth is that we are light beings, connected in oneness and unity, and we must lead the way in all areas of life with such integrity.

When your soul is ready to embody the light of Aries, you must look at all areas in your life that are asking you to be dynamic, brave, bold, vibrant, and lead the way regarding what truly aligns with your soul's mission. You must surrender to shining the light on the most empowered parts of your identity and carry this through into your work, relationships, and lifestyle.

Everything begins with our identity – here is the place where we must get to the bottom of truly knowing the self and what we would like to create in this lifetime. Everything starts with the self and we must recognise that before we can move forward into the 2nd house of Taurus.

Soul Communication

❖ What areas of your life are you shining a light on your soul's identity?
❖ What areas of your life is your soul's identity trapped in the shadows?
❖ Are you clear on who you are and exactly what you want to achieve in this lifetime?

Let us journey through the cyclic dimension to understand the power of cyclic nature and how this is one of the greatest gifts of being human.

CHAPTER 2

THE CYCLIC DIMENSION

"Every single one of us is traversing an endless cyclic journey, through the ever-unfolding magic of soulful evolution."

If we are to flow through the cyclic process of rebirth and create newness in our life, then we must first be dedicated to love.

For quite some years, there have been elements of unknown territory stirring in the depths of the collective soul of humanity. It is as if we have become caught up in a whirlwind of uncertainty, which is forcing us to forge a new path in life. We have reached the beginning stages of a global awakening that is calling every single one of us to go through the process of rebirthing the soul.

This is our unique call to remember unconditional love in all forms, as well as the power of oneness, healing and unity. Any type of rebirth that is attempting to take place within the soul can often create inner turmoil if rejected, denied or resisted. But change must happen, for change is the only constant in life.

With mental health concerns on the rise over the last decade, I believe it is vital for the collective to unite, remembering the power of oneness, community, and what can be born from the kindness of helping one another. I also believe that mental illness is not a negative experience but rather, it is the process of a sensitive soul tapping into the collective unconsciousness, where all repressed parts of oneself have been hidden for most of their life, without never truly being aware of this. They are being called to go through the journey of rebirth. They are being called to become the creator of their own life.

The more we resist, the harder it becomes. Essentially, rebirth is when we discover that we are shaped by a multidimensional universe and that anything is possible. We are not broken by mental health issues. Instead, we are discovering that our thoughts create our reality. We are discovering that all power comes from the mind, and so we must heal and re-program all fear through turning the unconscious into conscious energy, so that we are truly aware of the parts that we have repressed, rejected and denied. Rebirth is about the path to individuation; the path to owning all parts of the self.

Tapping into the collective unconsciousness occurs when one becomes completely aware of the changes that need making in their life. These changes are often conceptualising our identities that require reshaping and reforming, so that we can elevate higher and step into the most authentic version of ourselves.

I believe that 'mental illness' has become mistaken for the psychological, emotional, and spiritual process of rebirthing the soul – a cyclic transition that is inevitable.

However, change is coming, and we are all beginning to recognise that there is no help in battling such circumstances. Self-love is the answer because this is a far more empowering solution which enables surrender to effortlessly unfold within the soul. When we surrender to the old, new and positive manifestations arrive in divine timing and life begins to flow.

Rebirth is an ongoing journey since it is our call for the need to evolve in all areas of our life. It is no surprise that so many resist cyclic transitions, often feeling stuck in the wrong places due to fear of moving forward and surrendering to change. We lost the language of the soul through the dark ages when the goddess of divine feminine nature was forced into retreat. We live in fear of endings, but the truth is that there are never really endings – there is always a beginning of something new on the way. The reality is rebirthing the soul by letting go of the old ways that no longer serve us will always guide us to a new and far more exciting mission that is aligned with love.

As we move into the golden age of sheer light, we are slowly remembering the language of unity, love, and oneness. We are remembering because this language is our birth-right – it always has been and always will be. We remember this language when we start communicating through the essence of the infinite soul. That means doing what you love and doing it often so that you become aligned with your highest vibrational frequency.

The collective unification has already been initiated. I know this because I have already experienced the power of unity within my own life.

Through my journey of reshaping my identity over the last three years, I recognised how we have been living in a time where humans have become conditioned to try and 'make it alone.' I realised this concept through my own experience of being a lost soul trying to 'make it on my own.'

This programming of belief systems about trying to be the hero who does absolutely everything, has been handed down to us through the system of patriarchy. It is no longer working since it is delivering an illusion that is out of balance through its disconnection from the feminine. We must healthily lead the way with balance between both dimensions. We must remember that the best leadership happens when both the patriarchal and matriarchal essence are united. That means, being in balance between being a leader and being part of the community.

Individualism is excellent – I am not here to state that we are all the same – we are far from that. We are unique souls living subjective experiences; however, the old ways of the patriarchal system are crumbling as a new energy is being born into the world.

This new energy is rising from the divine nature of the feminine dimension which rejoices in the power of oneness, unity, and the balance between giving and receiving. This new energy is what is endeavouring to be born within the current collective unconsciousness. This new energy is expansive, creative, emotional and runs deep. This new energy brings us to a place of the unknown which is why it can often be mistaken for a stigmatised topic known as 'mental illness.' It is labelled as a problem when, in fact, it is a chance to rebirth the soul and an opportunity to significantly shift identity into an equilibrium between the masculine and feminine dimension. A sense of balance between logic and intuition, thought and emotion.

Firstly, it is not an illness or a problem. Shamanic traditions refer to this experience as a 'spiritual emergence' which is recognised within their culture as the initiation of a healer birthing new responsibility that they must embody. Journeying through a new cycle happens so that they can bring the wisdom back to the community to help others.

Rather than referring to this concept as 'mental illness' or 'spiritual emergence,' I am going to call it 'rebirth.' I have had my own experience of the western medicine model as well as working with Amazonian plant medicine. I will always be in a deep state of gratitude for how these medicines have helped me along the way. Both have been a blessing for what they provide and there is no right or wrong. They are equally important in this world. I must state that both provide beautiful ways to help a soul to go through its evolutionary process of rebirth. However, there are many other holistic ways to overcome such fear, rather than solely relying on medicating. Only when we can communicate on the soul level, can we begin to understand that rebirth is one of the most magnificent experiences any person can have, if they surrender to the emotions that rise to the surface.

Resistance to rebirth keeps you trapped in old limiting patterns that no longer serve your highest good. Surrendering to renewal expands you into a new state of consciousness so that you can become aligned with the unconditional love of the soul.

The soul holds the wisdom of journeying for thousands upon thousands of lifetimes. Your soul is always guiding you to live your most authentically aligned life. Your soul will always bring everything to you in divine timing, through a distinctive partnership with the universe. Whether you feel off track or on record, the truth is, wherever you are on your path, there are always signs in place that are endeavouring to guide you to the ever-unfolding process of being reborn.

In this new paradigm shift, we must remember and hold the vision in our hearts that nobody needs to be left behind, but rather, we each become an unwavering vibration of resilience, together. We can all live in a state of unconditional love, joy, prosperity, and abundance.

If the world needs anything right now, unconditional love is undoubtedly the answer. The love you have for yourself is a direct reflection of the love you have for others and Mother Earth, the planet we call home. So, make your home a beautiful place – make your inner world aligned with your outer world through surrendering to letting go of that which no longer serves you and opening to receive the new.

Soul Communication

❖ Are you ready to collect the key to your soul's blueprint?
❖ Are you ready to discover the power and wisdom that is waiting to be accessed in your heart?

❖ Are you ready to surrender to your cyclic nature so that you can live in wholeness, joy, abundance, and prosperity?

The beginning of one's quest requires stripping away many old and outdated layers of identities. These layers are the conditioning of outmoded mental patterns and belief systems that no longer serve a higher purpose. Releasing old programming is not only a mental detox, but a spiritual detox too. This newness is here to support you in the reshaping of both your inner and outer worlds, so that you can thrive in all areas of your life.

Through enthusiasm and openness to self-transformation, you are saying a huge yes to more health, wellbeing, passion, love and creativity. You are opting for valuable relationships, and an abundant lifestyle as well as a career that thrives. You are saying yes to having it all because you believe that it is possible to have it all through simply choosing an abundance mindset.

The straightforward yet profoundly influential exercises that I have created in this book are here to assist you in forging your new magical path. You can go wherever your heart desires to go and get creative with your manifestations. These are fundamental tools that are required to integrate the power of both mind and body alignment, with the soul. I have used these implements in my own life, and the process transcended some of my darkest, most fearful moments into the deepest of love and creativity.

Humanity must be willing to take the road less travelled if they would like to make a change. First with themselves. When one heals themselves, they heal the entire collective.

It is your willingness to evolve that will make this planet a healthier, safer, more loving, joyful, and caring place for us to live. After all, it is the only home we truly have so we must take care of this sacred place.

Please note that whatever nourishes you through your transition and change, you must do. Be sure to follow through with the things that nurture your soul. Take the candle-lit bath. You can book in for the remedial massage if you wish to. Meditate often. Visit a healer, therapist or mentor if needed. Whatever your mind, body and soul need to remain in a state of self-love, be sure to reach out and utilise these tools.

I believe that through your imperfections, you will find your authentic beauty. I believe that through your fears, you discover your greatest gifts.

I believe that through your demons, you will meet with your angels. Through solitude, you will find your best friend. And finally, through pain, you will find your greatest strength.

Mental illness is not so much about problems that arise in the mind. Instead, it is a rebirthing process that endures a deeply profound experience in connecting to the delicate, yet powerful web of universal consciousness. When one becomes aware of their thoughts, they tap into the duality of the mind, be it darkness or light. It is important to allow the energy of all thoughts to be release through non-attachment to whatever arises. When one is in a state of no thought, they have attained connection with their true nature – their soul. We can use meditation to set intentions of entering the heart space and embodying the vibration of unconditional love.

If somebody becomes aware of their thoughts, it means they are becoming aware that they are the creator of their own life. It also means that they can tap into everything they once believed to be accurate and release such limiting beliefs to create a new story – live a completely different reality. It is not so much a case of diminishing these thoughts or attempting to repress, deny or reject them. It is a chance to uncover the messages that are coming through, and an opportunity to transcend old programming of fear to more love and alignment. In the process of going through a rebirthing cycle, it is so vital that we are all dedicated to unconditional love.

During my journey of battling with the resistance to rebirth, I found that one of the most potent forces was the love that I received from my family who held me in my darkest moments. They allowed me to be me, rather than focusing on the fact that I was potentially 'broken' and needed 'fixing'. They knew I was undergoing the process of learning a newfound language of the soul and that I had to surrender to all change. Receiving this unconditional love was one of the most powerful experiences I have ever had in my entire life, and I hope that you too, can also transcend your fears into the greatest of love.

By understanding that any crisis is not about battling or fighting and trying to overcome, but instead surrendering to what is possible and knowing that it is more so a lesson about love, we can feel liberated by the journey of rebirthing the soul and transforming the mind.

Let me take you on a journey through light, guided towards the ancient wisdom of the spirit and the callings of your soul. This ancient wisdom holds a divine purpose for waking up to the magic of this beautiful universe. This journey is not linear; it is cyclic. Perhaps understanding cyclic nature through this story may give you the permission to step into your intuitive and empathic abilities, breaking free from the rigidity that the logical world has had humanity trapped in for aeons of time.

I would also like to make a great emphasis on the importance of self-love and self-care throughout this book. Due to the suffering that lack of self-love and self-care once created for me, I almost did not make it to where I am today. I probably would not be writing this book which means you would not be reading it. I share this story from the most vulnerable depths of my heart – not just so that I can learn to love the parts of myself that were once fragmented, but so that you too can integrate the fragmented pieces of your identities. They are calling out for healing and change.

Wholeness knocks on the door of a deeply courageous heart. Wholeness is a journey for brave souls, since courage is the very thing that teaches one to face their fears. Brave hearts are like lions who live with strength but remain open to receiving pure love. This journey is not for those who are unwilling to surrender and let go of everything they hold onto that no longer serves them. This is an exciting mission for those who trust in the power of love.

CHAPTER 3

YOUR SOUL'S IDENTITY

"I open to receive the magic of my soul's most authentic identity."

Soul Communication

❖ What does soul connection mean?

❖ Is it something we can understand beyond logic?

❖ And how can we utilise this connection to being guided along our highest path?

Being connected through the soul is being connected to the all-giving source of life. It is fusing to dimensions that are beyond the five senses. While we are all one consciousness riding one big magnetic wave, your soul speaks its unique language and has its very own beautiful expression.

Being connected to the soul beautifully exemplifies the paradox of life itself. The paradox is that we are everything as well as nothing. Our soul speaks its own language and we can also have moments of remembering things in strange ways. De-Jah-Vu moments. It is as if our soul plugs into something that the mind simply cannot comprehend. I believe that De-Jah-Vu happens when we come back onto the path of our most divine calling; when we return to exactly where we are supposed to be – alignment.

You can strengthen your inner compass through the practice of conscious heart chakra connection. This energy centre is the link between grounding energies of the root chakra, sacral chakra, and solar plexus, while expanding the awareness of the crown chakra, third eye and throat chakra. The heart is the active centre of universal source – all-giving, all-receiving flow of love.

Creating a separation between our energy and the earth is the very thing that forms the sickness of the soul. However, if we soak up the wilderness of nature from time to time, we can open our chakras, connecting to the roots of the divine Mother Earth. As we receive her free-flowing healing energy, the Sacred Mother, provides our rights to recharge.

Sometimes, it is great to take off our shoes and fully ground our energies. I know it's impossible to walk around without shoes all day – I am not saying give up your shoes – but instead, take time to touch the earth with your bare feet even if it's once a week. Known as 'earthing', this a great topic and there is plenty of information out there for you to educate yourself.

We too can consciously choose to be open to heightened awareness through the practice of asking and receiving downloads. The newness, insight, and creativity accessed through meditation and connection to the divine father – universe – is what brings about change and zest for new adventures in life. Draw upon these two worlds of mother earth and father universe, integrating both concepts into everyday life, and through such heart-based living, you will be guided to seeing the life-giving source of spirit in everyone and everything.

Each time we consciously choose to let the divinity of mother and father unite within the very centre of the heart; we say yes to igniting the essence of soul as well as activating positive energy flow. This integration of polarity not only heals one from the inside out but acts as an immensely powerful tool for achieving presence and being the cheerleader of your own life.

Since we are often more than not caught up in the stress of pushing and striving in both career and lifestyle, it is no surprise to witness so many of us feeling disconnected from the mother and father source. If we are to recover all the lost parts of ourselves and anchor in the truth of our equilibrium, we must be willing to let success be defined simply as 'a state of wellbeing'.

You see, the universe loves to support us. It does not have some cunning plan to suddenly stop giving to us one day, nor is it waiting for us to fail and suffer. In any given moment we can reach out to the universe and ask for something different in our life if change is what we desire. We hold power to make such a change. In freeing ourselves from the chains of everyday stresses that keep us locked in an unnecessary prison, the universe will always step in to help. All we must do is ask.

Soul Communication

❖ What stories are you playing over in your subconscious mind?
❖ Is your story about love and abundance or fear and lack?
❖ Are you aware that the thoughts you send out will return because it is the laws of the universe to respond?

In June 2017, I was sitting in my candle-lit bedroom in my apartment at Sydney Olympic Park, Australia. I had been going through the turbulent waters of my inner darkness for quite some time, feeling trapped in the wrong relationship. It had become outdated, and I was no longer engaged in my soul's blueprint. I had a high paid job as a copywriter, I had an incredible number of friends around me, and my home was the most beautiful sanctuary, but my relationship was on the verge of breaking down.

I wanted to hold onto everything I had attained because I lived in Australia thanks to my partner, sponsoring me on a de facto visa. But the truth is that you cannot force love. He had broken free from his shell, living a life in the music industry, and while it was fun for the first few years of our relationship, I felt like I could no longer show up to a life of drugs and partying each weekend. I was once using this as a mode of escapism, but it was no longer serving me. It was my way of avoiding my inner calling, but I no longer could feed my emptiness.

We had been moving in separate directions for almost one year, trying to show up to the relationship with integrity. Still, my soul craved to spread its wings because I could no longer force something that felt totally out of alignment.

Winter had arrived in the southern hemisphere, and all I felt called to do was meditate. Little did I know that I was being called by my ancestors to transmute this darkness to light. I had a long journey ahead of me.

Sat there, in a profoundly peaceful meditation, which I often retreated to when my partner was out with friends, I met one of the most fearful belief systems that live in the human psyche. The intention I had placed on this meditation was to be guided to a state of stillness so that my soul could emerge and give me some guidance on where I was to transition with life. I needed this because I there were internal wounds that needed to be healed and released. This was the start of a huge journey into the underworld, to reclaim my own healing of both body and mind, thanks to the guided wisdom of my soul, that came here to do this work in this lifetime.

Moving from peaceful stillness to this fearful belief system, I felt my internal world shake and crumble. It was as if I received the energy that was feeling trapped by my grandmother, who took her own life back in 1974. Suicide is not the most peaceful topic in the world, so when this terrifying energy came over me, I jumped up from my seated position, and felt this instant rush of pain surge throughout my body. *"I am you, and you are me – we are one,"* my soul cried. I felt the words ripple through me as if I had received a startling message from the entire universe. I started to cry. I looked at myself in the mirror with complete surrender and felt the fears that live in the collective consciousness. It was time to heal my ancestral lineage. It was time to embark on a journey of healing the mind through freeing and releasing this trapped energy.

I cried for quite some time. I felt the pain rippling through me about the labels and fear that was associated not only with death, but with the act of taking one's own life. The shame, the blame, the anger, the resentment. All the darkest emotions that create the label around suicide.

At this moment in time, I could feel her heart beating alongside mine. I could feel the intense suffering of her need to be free from the mental struggles and anxiety that caused her to take her own life. She had become so disconnected from the unconditional love of the soul that she felt trapped. However, after my rebirthing journey, I can now safely say this energy no longer lives within my ancestral lineage. As we heal ourselves, we heal our ancestors and also heal our future children.

As humans, we must release old identities that no longer serve us. We must free them with love and open space for recreating and reshaping our world, designed by love and compassion.

When suicide runs in the family lineage, the next generation carries the pain and trauma from womb to womb. So, it is no surprise that the rebirthing process has been a difficult topic for my mother after what happened to her mother. I know this because it took me decades to free myself from the shadows, transmuting this process of darkness to light through surrendering to the very thing I – and most people – would prefer to reject, deny and avoid.

The truth is that you cannot push away death, and you certainly cannot drive away suicide by labelling it as a mental illness. The more one rejects and shoves away into the shadows, the more profound pain it will cause. The more we label mental illness as something problematic, the more we will resist the process of rebirth.

One of the worst mistakes that I made during the process of being called to be reborn was the resentment that I had attached to my grandfather's actions and how he could have done differently in his relationship with my grandmother. How he could have treated her better during her times of struggle and perhaps her suicide would never have happened. This belief system was one of my mother's in which I carried — my aunt's too. I had to learn to let go of holding onto other people's blame.

Blame is not the answer. If past pain travels from womb to womb, let it also be said that belief systems move from mindset to mindset. Only when I was able to stop carrying my mother's belief systems surrounding blame and resentment was I able to forgive my grandfather for his inability to show up with a dedicated heart. I accept his path because he did not have the tools to deal with such circumstances, and that is all there is to it. I forgive both my grandmother and grandfather for their journeys because they have a reason for them. Rather than looking at the responsibility of healing as a burden, I now embody it as a gift. Our ancestors also pass on incredibly beautiful and positive traits, and we must focus our attention on those.

We all have different tools in the bag. Every single one of our souls holds wisdom in various measures dependent on the experiences we have had, the parents who shaped us as children, the partners we have been with, and the work we do in the world. We are all designed differently, but one thing we must remember is that we are all connected to the divinity of the soul, and love is the language of our birth-right.

It was only at the beginning of 2020 in which I finally recognised that I had become my most authentic self, searching for the deepest inquires that my soul needed to express. For decades, I had not only carried the call for rebirth in my soul that was associated with my mother's line, but I had taken, from a young age, specific belief systems within the masculine dimension, that was associated with my father's line.

We must release our parent's identities and belief systems that no longer serve a purpose. We must carry through their wisdom with love and let their light continue to live on through us. My mother, a September Virgo, is a medicine woman who has been through a life of shamanic initiations but never indeed answered the call. It is my job to answer this call and carry the gift of our intuitive feminine skill of nurture and healing. My father, a November Sagittarius, is a born leader who has been very humbly successful with life but pushed himself to the brink of burnout to get to where he is today. It is my job to continue his legacy of humbling success with a sense of nourishment, knowing that success does not have to be overwhelming, complicated, or stressful.

I have four sisters, three of which are Aries. Growing up with three Aries sisters has always created a lot of passion and fire in the family. This fire has taught me the power that lives in shaping the soul's identity and how important it is to do so with love.

My sisters are incredible reflections of the light elements that are born from the house of Aries. One of the twins is dynamic with her approach to work, while the other reflects a bold character in terms of fashion and the way she shows up with her physical appearance every day.

Tia is six years younger than myself, yet I have always looked towards her as a leader, just as she looks towards me as a leader too. Together, we have been through so much. This sisterhood of pure love is what puts the fire in my heart to write this book. Without Tia, I probably would not have found the courage to step up and share this story, so thank you for your Aries fire and inspiration.

Aries energy is potent medicine. When we are focusing on our identities, we must first look around at the state of the world and where others need us because the house of Aries calls us to step up. To step up and be leaders for ourselves and others. If we lack inspiration with our work, then it is time to use the fire to create a more authentic career that aligns with the soul. If we are wearing the same colour clothes each day, then it is time to spruce up the wardrobe with a variety of colour that expresses the soul's energy. If we are hiding away from our most authentic truth, afraid of speaking up about what truly matters to us, then it is time to use the fire to step up and become the leader we need to be in the world.

Soul Communication

- ❖ How does your soul's identity shape your work and career?
- ❖ How does your soul's identity shape your physical appearance?
- ❖ Where in your life do you need to transcend the shadows of Aries?
- ❖ Where in your life do you need to call on the light of Aries?

Your inner guide is here to help you manifest all that you would like to have in your life. But first, this requires a shift in thinking. It requires relentlessly participating in the act of change and it also requires trust – a whole lot of trust.

We cannot fix things with the same thinking that created the initial problem. Sometimes it can feel strange to re-train the mind when it has been so used to the same cycle of stories. This can be a challenge, but once we have cultivated a habit of positive thoughts and affirmations, this new habit can work with the energy of the soul and set change into motion. I must also express that we must only use the mind when needed, for our manifestations – we also need time out to simply be free from the psychological realm and not attached to our thoughts. This is where meditation, stillness and peace of mind come into play.

We can be the conscious creators of change by simply choosing a new set of thoughts and, in the process, healing cellular memory. To transcend fear to faith and move from ego-based thinking to soul, we must find the strength to affirm, I am, I can and I will.

Next time you find yourself slipping back into old patterns, allow your higher self to arise in all its fullness. Allow your soul to bring forward this infinite strength. Your soul knows that stories shaped around scarcity and fear are just a made-up illusion created by the ego to protect oneself. Your soul is here to serve you. It is here to remind you that none of this is true, for we can only allow it to become our reality if we give meaning to it.

Become aware of where you are giving your power away to old beliefs and ideas. Know that you can change this. How will you tap into this change? Self-awareness. Awareness is the key.

Soul Communication

- ❖ Are you ready to embody the purest form of self-love?
- ❖ Ready to transcend old limiting beliefs so that you can recreate a new, beautifully abundant reality?

With a little discipline, you can work with the mind and body, integrating the essence of soul. You can activate your incredible healing journey towards alignment of the soul, by simply altering your thoughts so that they align with the callings of your heart.

CHAPTER 4

THE 1ˢᵀ SOUL COMMUNICATION

"When I set my heart on my intentions, the universe delivers."

Take a moment to fill in the blank spaces below. Upon completion, find a quiet area to be with the infinity of your soul and read your intentions out loud so that your mind can align with these intentions and your body can sink into the feeling that these objectives bring.

Let these goals remain firm in your heart and leave the rest in the hands of the universe.

Olivia Blakey

I, _____ *, across time and space, choose now, to set the intention of*

_____
_____
_____
_____
_____
_____
_____
_____

I choose to feel

_____
_____
_____
_____
_____
_____
_____
_____
_____

I would like to be guided towards

_____
_____

_____

_____

_____

_____

_____

_____

_____

_____

I am ready for

_____

_____

_____

_____

_____

_____

_____

_____

_____

_____

I am open to receiving things such as

_____

_____

_____

_____

_____

_____

_____

_____

_____

_____

I believe this is the path my soul is calling me towards, because

_____

_____

_____

_____

_____

_____

_____

_____

_____

I am dedicated to all the above and focus my intention on this vibration, allowing all that is for my highest good to come through. I am open to my soul showing me, guiding me, and strengthening my connection to all that I am. Across time and space, I, choose now to walk the path of my greatest potential.

My soul will support me in making my dreams reality, returning to my birth-right of wholeness, and living a life of love, joy, abundance, and creativity.

Signed

_____

Dated

_____

"There will always be ancient wisdom in the soul that is waiting to be discovered. Find your wisdom and you will become the creator of your most authentic life."

What do you believe your soul's purpose is in this lifetime?

You can include everything that you have achieved/overcome or feel called to accomplish in the future – from health and wellness to relationships, finances, lifestyle, and career. There is no right or wrong answer – what matters is that you follow your soul because it knows the way.

My soul's purpose is

_____

_____

_____

_____

_____

_____

_____

_____

_____

_____

_____

_____

_____

_____

CHAPTER 5

THE BULL

"I have everything I need, and I am completely grateful for all of it."

Sign: Taurus
Ruler: Venus
Element: Earth
Season: Spring
Colour: Green
Stone: Emerald
Light elements: Down-to-earth, Generous, Honest, Kind, Loyal
Shadow elements: Defensive, Greedy, Hostile, Stubborn, Possessive

The 2nd house in astrology takes us on a journey through the 3rd dimension, which represents all ownership of materialism in the physical realm. It is everything that belongs to us during our time on planet earth. It is our connection to belonging, love, and how we take care of our physicality, our finances and everything we own. It is a strong representation of the home and how this place is our sanctuary – not just where we live on the earth, but the body in which our soul is housed in.

We must honour all the physical elements of life with love and appreciation if we are to stand in the light – the positive aspects – of the house of Taurus.

The journey through the 2nd house asks us to become masters of taking great care of the physical realm. With its connection to everything in the material, it is undoubtedly a reflection of how we take care of our bodies, and the foods we eat to stay nourished. Not only is this house a metaphor for the physical body, it has a strong association with the work we do in the world to create our financial income, and where we choose to circulate this currency.

When we are in the elements of the bull's light, we are entirely grateful for everything we have and own. We feel that we are given everything we truly need and that our soul is always providing us with the right tools in divine timing. This does not just apply to belongings (such as a car or the house we own), but the deepest of connections to love too. The question is not so much how deep your love is, but rather, how much love are you allowing into your life?

Often, being stuck in rigid and limited ways of thinking, with a story that is shaped by old programming and belief systems means that one is trapped in the shadow elements of the bull when it comes to everything physically speaking. Being defensive, greedy, hostile, stubborn, and possessive is often correlated with having and attaining too much in life with little appreciation.

When we travel through this house, we are asked to bring out the appreciation of a minimalist within ourselves. Someone who is in alignment with their soul will probably achieve a lot in their life, but they are light-workers who recognise and appreciate that everything is simply borrowed here on the earth, in this lifetime.

Those who can live in simplicity or are super generous and giving when they tend to have abundance in their lives are most probably down-to-earth, generous, honest, kind, and loyal souls. They are living in the light of the bull and are in total appreciation of the love and beauty that the physical realm can bring and how balancing the act of giving and receiving is a truly valuable goal in life.

Each day that I write this book I am surrounded by the beauty, love and belonging of Taurus energy. This theme has always run strongly throughout my family, with my grandmother on my father's side being a Taurus, my brother's beautiful partner and many close friends. It is no surprise that I manifested my twin soul who is also a Taurus – he is symbolic of a strong earth element with a resilient outlook on life, grounding my dreamy, watery, spiritual Piscean energy into the physical realm.

While he keeps the foundations of balance within my life, he also lets me be in my creative flow and fly with my wildest dreams. That is why I am so grateful to journey through the house of Taurus, because it really teaches you the joys of combining water and earth elements. Integrating spirit and matter.

Together, my soulmate and I are constantly anchoring spirit into matter and that is what I appreciate most about this house – it is a place where you can recognise the process of manifestation and all dreams coming into existence. Here you not only hold the deepest of gratitude for all that you already have, but also you can recognise the magic that is possible in transforming spirit into matter. This magic happens through simply choosing conscious thoughts and aligning with the mission and blueprint of the soul. Holding the vision and taking the action is the best recipe for manifestation.

Those who are connected to the energy of the bull are seriously great at manifesting spiritual creativity into matter. This is because they are so deeply connected to the physical realm and all its beauty. Since the bull is symbolic of the 3rd dimension, and all that lives in the physical world, it is a powerful medicine for creating heaven on earth, not only in our relationships, but at home, within our bodies and the work that we do.

When I left Australia and made my way to New Zealand, I could feel my Taurus grandmother guiding me to a new life of unconditional love. I had lost my home as well as my career and relationships. Although she had died in 2012, I could feel her energy in the astral realm, guiding me to recreate a sanctuary, since the concept of home is quite possibly our most vital element of life. Everything begins with the home, not just the place in which we live but how we treat our bodies.

After travelling around the north island of New Zealand, I made the decision to settle on the west coast just in time for Christmas with some wonderful housemates, living near the ocean. The stillness that lived in my new home was beautiful. I woke up to the birds singing each morning and could feel their songs reflecting the start of something new.

The soul is always ready to welcome the newness of the physical dimension. I had been living out of alignment for far too long and this was my chance to become a vibrational match of love, starting with a new, blank slate.

When we are journeying through the physical dimension, we must not become attached to that which we 'own' on earth. It is said that we do not inherit the earth from our ancestors, but rather, we borrow it from our children.

January 2018 was the beginning of my deepest and darkest journey through the shadows of my own fears and unease with life. I had become completely attached to everything that I had to let go of. I felt angry that I had lost my previous home, with little appreciation for my new home. My mind was trapped in an endless battle – not towards anyone or anything, but towards myself. It was difficult to surrender.

I fell into a deep depression in February 2018 and this lasted a few weeks. It was by far the worst few weeks of my life because although my soul was attempting to fully surrender, I was instead holding onto the pains of the past within my mind. I had no inspiration to turn up to work at the new job I had just attained in Auckland. I had no inspiration to see friends or explore new places. I had completely lost all my energy for life itself and the only thing that would soothe my soul was being out in the heart of nature. When we do not have the inspiration to show up, we are deeply asked to transform the inner emptiness and learn to be grateful for what we have whilst we are working for what we want. The truth is that we can rebuild tomorrow with today's heart of gratitude.

Three years on, I have utterly understood the power of gratitude and how it enables one to move mountains when they recognise it in all areas of their life. If we are not grateful for what we have then how do we expect more to arrive in our lives?

When I escalated into that dark hole, I lost a lot of sleep from my stress levels that were skyrocketing through the roof. I am so deeply grateful that my parents came out to New Zealand to bring me home during the inner turmoil my mindset went through because I felt so disconnected from life that I couldn't possibly make the right decisions for myself. I had to fully surrender and hand over the reins of holding on. I had to let go and press the reset button. I had to go through the process of rebirth by returning to my family home in the north of England and start over.

So, I returned, and I went into my own retreat.

Starting over was by far the wisest move I ever made. When I gathered myself after quite some time, I journeyed back through the process of reshaping my soul's identity and becoming more aligned with my heart's mission. I used many of the exercises in this book which brings me to where I am today. Currently, I am in a deep space of self-love, learning that I am worthy of everything I would like to attain in this lifetime. I am learning that we must set intentions with the mind, but feeling and embodying the frequency of unconditional love is the most powerful force in the universe. It took me many years to recover from the darkest moments but I am by far, the most resilient I have ever been in my entire life. The darkness should not be pushed away. We should listen to what it is asking from us because usually our inner darkness is attempting to guide us in changing for the better.

We all go through the highs and the lows. The problems in our life are not problems – they are preparing us for what is ahead. I know this because I am stronger now than I ever have been in my entire life. I know what works for me and I know what does not work for me. I am certain that the same applies to you. Not just in terms of relationships with others, but the relationship with myself. Not just in terms of my career, but in terms of my home and my entire environment. I know what does and does not work in terms of everything, and yet the paradox is this – I know nothing. For the more I learn, the less I seem to know. The more I surrender to this, the better my life will unfold – and yours too. This is because we are all students and teachers in life. We are everything and yet we are nothing. That is my wisdom, born from the house of Taurus and I embody that magic onto my life path every single day.

Soul Communication

- ❖ What elements of the bull's light are reflected in your life?
- ❖ What elements of the bull's shadow are reflected in your life?
- ❖ Do you have unconditional love and appreciation for everything that belongs to you in the physical realm?

CHAPTER 6

THE PHYSICAL DIMENSION

"When you connect with the magic of your inner world, you create potential in your outer world."

"You will find me in your deepest pain, and you will find me in your greatest joy. You will find me in your tears of sorrow and the sunshine in your smiles. You will know me when you find me because you will understand that every emotion serves a purpose. You will know when you find me because I am you and you are me – we are one." – Mother Earth.

Your soul is calling – it always has been, and it always will be. The higher vibration of feminine energy that is currently upgrading on the earth is a message from the divine feminine dimension. This energy is asking you to comfortably rise in the skin of your own glorious divinity. This energy is asking you to do so by understanding how the soul communicates through its calling. This energy is asking you to learn the language of the soul that was once lost.

Through surrendering to the temporarily uncomfortable process of 'stripping away the old', the entire globe is going through the shedding of the snakeskin phase, rebirthing a new connection to the way we live our lives on this planet.

We are moving away from a sense of separation and competition; aligning with a higher frequency that is oneness and collaboration. This is precisely what is happening in the depths of our souls right now, and we must surrender to all of it.

As we sail through the evolutionary waves of the soul, we often encounter moments of discomfort. This uneasiness can leave us in a state of resisting, and preferably, we hold onto the familiar, choosing to fear what might be ahead waiting in the unknown.

If you are to feel any resistance, then this is a direct message from your soul for you to surrender at all costs. For it is our belief systems that block us from attaining the gold that is waiting to be discovered within our hearts. Removing the programming around fear can only happen when we focus our intention on the things we love and are most grateful for.

The physical realm is always journeying through cycles. Cyclic nature requires both ends of the scale – to live for the new and to die to the old. We too must allow ourselves to surrender in releasing old ways whilst we are alive, so that we can be reborn. Only can the newness be born when we are liberated from old programming that is limited and no longer serves us.

Often, the people who are dedicated to forging new paths tend to feel like black sheep, alienated in a world that seems a little strange for the human spirit to be part of.

These are the people quitting the daily grind of 9 to 5 jobs that feel as if they are a road to nowhere. These are the people who recognise that their creativity is more valuable and far wealthier than working in a mundane role that does not compliment the spirit of humanity.

These people also know that they can be extremely wealthier through utilising their creative outlet, rather than solely relying on income from elsewhere. These people manifest their dreams from within rather than being controlled by outer circumstances.

These are the people buying one-way tickets across the globe to reignite the adventure that was once denied in their soul; to recreate their lives by meeting new people and exploring new places. These people know that travel is one of the most excellent teachers of journeying both inner and outer worlds.

But most of all, these are the people who have discovered that there is a far more profound way to heal themselves. These are the people who channel their shadow elements of self into a creative outlet, transcending darkness to light and fear to love. These are the people who follow their truth, for they do not deny any part of themselves, but rather, integrate all elements of the setbacks and achievements to move forward and live in complete wholeness. These people own all parts of themselves with complete integrity.

If you are completing this workbook then you are certainly one of these people – feeling like a black sheep can often feel like a curse, but rather, these people have creative gifts and operate in a completely dynamic paradigm.

Let me make it clear that it is okay if you have no idea why you are here doing this work. Know that you do not have to know everything. Know that your higher self is soon to weave together the thread that makes total sense. Through your dedication in taking the step forward by intentionally manifesting your newly aligned inner and outer worlds, you are already moving closer to the love, joy, creativity and abundance that is your birth-right.

Your soul is probing you to relentlessly find the strength to go through the process of metaphorical death and rebirth. Do not be frightened by this however, for the metamorphosis in which your inner alchemy will bring forth, is an entirely new world waiting to be uncovered – magic in its purest form.

Soul Communication

- ❖ Are you willing to surrender to such an opportunity of coming home to yourself?
- ❖ Are you ready to walk your soul's path, live your purpose and embrace your destiny?
- ❖ Do you believe that the universe will move mountains for you when you finally choose your alignment?
- ❖ How are you showing up to act in manifesting spirit into matter?
- ❖ Do you believe that the universe has your back?

Allow yourself to relentlessly participate in anchoring the callings of your soul, for here you will meet with your inner knowing and your most beautiful wisdom. Here you will be called to your bliss by this universal language of love.

CHAPTER 7

HOME

"When we drop the reins of control and begin to follow what lights up the soul, we set health, career, relationships, and lifestyle into an ever-flowing motion of abundance. Abundance is our birth-right. Our home."

One of the reasons why I struggled so much when I arrived in New Zealand was not just because I had come out of a toxic lifestyle, but because I felt like my entire home and foundations had been destroyed right in front of my eyes. Yes, I had my home and family back in the UK, nevertheless, I have always been the sort of person that wants to explore new realms and go travel to different places and really liberate my soul. Travel was what lit me up and I thought that this would be my medicine – but rebirth can often require rest and retreating within to nourish your inner world.

When I was travelling around New Zealand, I came to understand that the foundations that I had built previously meant so much to me that I just did not feel safe or secure wherever I stepped. I had my friends but felt so alone. I had a wonderful job but felt completely disconnected from the work I would do. I had a lot of great things in my life, but I was completely out of alignment with gratitude for the simple things. Rebirth calls for us to learn the deepest of gratitude. It is a superpower that guides us closer to the things that matter most to us. It is a superpower that enables us to stay healthy and happy, feeling in love with what we have. It is a superpower that grants us permission to manifest more of what we love in our life.

I tried so hard to maintain such a dynamic vision about setting up a new home. I really tried to set up a new life, but every single night when I went to bed, I could not help but feel this huge sense of sadness come through my body and soul. It rippled like a dark wave in the night. They say that home is where the heart is, but I was disconnected from my heart, and therefore I was not feeling at home with myself and my surroundings.

I was being called to go within and journey through my heart every single day to remember my own divinity and hold the deepest of gratitude for all that I had in my life. But I felt isolated and I felt lonely.

I had lost my zest for life and I had no idea which direction I was supposed to move in. I had no idea what path I was to now forge. I started learning the power of boundaries and how we must say a firm yes to what matters and a firm no to what does not serve us. I needed to learn boundaries because I had never had them in place until now. Boundaries are healthy because they determine how focused you are on what matters, and they also protect you from being consumed by the things that distract you from achieving your highest calling.

There was once a time when saying yes to and doing absolutely everything was classed as successful. Yes, quite literally, we have become beings who can claim a winner's prize for suffering the worst burn out of the year award. However, things are changing. Rapidly.

People are ditching the 9 to 5 to be their own boss. Travellers are buying one-way tickets, forging their spontaneous paths. Society is realising that you do not always need a bachelor's degree to become an entrepreneur. As a collective, we are fast discovering that success is supposed to come from a place of pleasure and that we must set boundaries, saying a firm no to what does not serve us.

When we choose to do things out of pressure, we can be sure that there is a 'should' involved. Doing things from a place of pressure is acting out of wounds, fears, scars, and pain. Pressure is driven by fear presented by the ego. But pressure cannot be enriching for the soul, and every single one of us knows this. Whether its work, career, finances, or generally the way you show up in the world, this must come from a place of pleasure – what lights up your soul. If the driving force is pressure, then it will not be long before you realise that you are swimming upstream, going against the current of life. You are truly home when you feel the pleasures of life, and if you focus on doing the things you love then the truth is that you will do it well.

Soul Communication

- ❖ Can we truly break free from the limitation of believing burnout equals success?
- ❖ How can we allow ourselves to live in an ever-expanding place of joy?
- ❖ What does home mean to you?
- ❖ Where do you do things out of pressure?
- ❖ Where do you do things out of pleasure?
- ❖ What boundaries do you have in place to protect your soul's gold?

CHAPTER 8

THE 2ND SOUL COMMUNICATION

"When I release all that which no longer serves me, I open up to receiving all that is waiting to be embodied."

Take a minute to sit in a quiet space. Close your eyes and connect with the stillness that waits to be accessed in the centre of your heart. If you need longer to tune in or have a preferred way of 'tuning in' then go ahead. Do what feels most aligned for you.

Now, focus on your breath and visualise a golden light within this deep space in your heart. This golden light is the essence of your soul. Here is the place of all-knowing, love, abundance, clarity, purpose, strength, and wisdom. There is no such thing as fear or doubt here – this is your divine light and know that you can access this at any given moment.

Once you have reached the seat of your soul, ask your higher self, *"To further evolve on my journey to infinite abundance, what needs to be released?"*

Sit here with this question. Be patient. Allow your soul's voice to come through with its guidance. Trust that this guidance is for your highest good.

Write a list of ten (can be less or more) things in your life that require releasing, for you to create new space in your life for inviting in a higher vibration of love.

Next to each point, write any uncomfortable emotions that surround the attachment to this belief, person or experience.

Soul Communication

- ❖ How does it make you feel to release these things?
- ❖ What reasons do you have for holding onto these things?
- ❖ What can you invite into your life once you release to create new space?

Let each emotion come to you and be held. Sit with each feeling for as long as needed. Allow yourself to fully sense these uncomfortable energies it may bring, knowing all emotions serve a purpose. Welcome each feeling into your energy field rather than resisting it. Know that this is only a temporary experience, and emotions are simply energy in motion.

Trust that when you surrender to allowing these emotions, you can begin to understand why you may hold onto belief systems and why they need to be released.

Remember, this is about getting comfortable with feelings, so they no longer hold power over you.

Now, write a list of ten (can be less or more) things that you would like to invite into your life to replace the old with the new. These things are aligned with your soul and attract more love and abundance into your life.

_____

_____

_____

_____

_____

_____

_____

_____

_____

_____

Upon completion, take a moment to write your affirmations. These require powerful words to empower you! Check out my example below.

Affirmation: *"I am supported in all that I do. My choices are perfect, and I will always be successful in following through with the things that light up my soul."*

_____

_____

_____

_____

_____

_____

_____

_____

_____

_____

Turn to your personalised affirmations and read out loud whenever experiencing moments of uncertainty. There is so much power in words – speak your affirmations with determination and know that it is the law of the universe to respond. By choosing a more loving and caring choice of thoughts, your mind can begin to work effortlessly with the callings of your soul.

"Breathe into fear long enough, and it will be transcended to love."

Write a list of all the things that make your soul sparkle in its glorious divinity. For example, hiking, painting, hitting the gym, going to the beach, coffee dates, baking, hanging out with friends, etc. Remember, there is no right or wrong, and you can dream as big and bold as desired. What matters is that you recognise where your alignment is.

_____

_____

_____

_____

_____

_____

_____

_____

_____

_____

How will doing more of these things nurture your mind, body and soul?

Mind

_____

_____

_____

_____

_____

_____

_____

_____

_____

Body

_____

_____

_____

_____

_____

_____

_____

_____

_____

Soul

_____

_____

_____

_____

_____

_____

_____

_____

_____

_____

If there is one thing you must know, this list is one of the most important lists you will ever write. Since everything begins with the self, you must become so powerfully aligned with what lights you up and positively energise your mind, body and soul.

You can update the list as you evolve. You can break the record down into areas of family, friends, career, and lifestyle, if you wish. The point is that you fulfil your journey with lots of moments on this list because this is where spiritual nourishment can indeed transpire.

CHAPTER 9

THE TWINS

*"I think my thoughts into existence; therefore,
I choose thoughts of love."*

Sign: Gemini
Ruler: Mercury
Element: Air
Season: Spring
Colour: Yellow
Stone: Tiger's Eye
Light elements: Adaptable, Cheerful, Friendly, Resourceful, Sociable
Shadow elements: Critical, Intrusive, Invasive, Shallow, Unpredictable

When we journey through the 3rd house of Gemini, we are travelling through the higher mind. This is not just the place of the higher mind, but of the ego and shadow too. The 3rd house asks us whether we are integrating all parts of ourselves or whether there are parts of our soul's identity that we shove into the shadows.

When one is living in the light of Gemini, their thoughts and belief systems are aligned with the callings of the heart. This is not just a place where we must recognise that we are manifesting our thoughts into existence; it is a place where we must be mindful about the thoughts we choose. Gemini reminds us that our thoughts create our reality.

The twins are a perfect example of how we must create a partnership between the ego and the shadow self. Rather than accepting some parts of our soul's identity and denying others, we must step into our wholeness of living, breathing and being all parts of oneself. We must be responsible for and take ownership of all elements of ourselves. We must transcend our deepest darkest shadows into the purest form of love and light.

Those who are feeling trapped in the shadows of the 3rd house will often reflect critical, intrusive, invasive, shallow, and unpredictable behaviour.

It is not because they are choosing to be this way, but rather, this is the reaction that unfolds when one does not claim all parts of their being. They are more than likely denying the shadow parts of themselves and putting a huge emphasis on the ego. To become whole, we must delve into a journey of shadow work which can often trigger a dark night of the soul. This is because the 3rd house teaches us to face the things, we do not necessarily like about ourselves. It teaches us to learn to love all elements through the power of soulful integration.

Whenever I am personally journeying through the 3rd house of the higher mind, I find that my shadow elements often include being judgemental, overthinking and highly self-critical. I learned to transcend this energy through painting. As soon as I put paintbrush to canvas, my shadows begin to transform into creativity – I can shift my perspective and discover that an overactive mind is calling to channel thoughts into art. This is my go-to every time I feel overwhelmed by the shadows that tend to creep in during stressful times in life.

What matters is that one finds a solution to channel their shadows. Whether it is dancing, art, baking, writing, singing, cleaning, producing music or any other medium. What matters is the journey from a place of resistance to love. Creating is a powerful way from shifting out of mind and into the heart. What you choose to create will often reflect your state of energy – sometimes my paintings are real dark, sometimes they are extremely bright. No judgement needs to be applied to the outcome. We must always be grateful for having many tools around us that help us to transform and shift energy.

Soul Communication

- ❖ What elements of the twin's light are reflected in your life?
- ❖ What elements of the twin's shadow are reflected in your life?
- ❖ How can you integrate your ego and shadow self so that you can become whole?
- ❖ Is the programming of your thoughts aligned with the unconditional love of your soul?

CHAPTER 10

THE PSYCHOLOGICAL DIMENSION

"When you hold the deepest of gratitude for all that you have, here and now, you open your heart to receiving infinite abundance from an unlimited source within the universe."

Humans repeat patterns over and over without realising. Often, it is not until they feel completely bored, low, or stuck that they decide to make a change and evolve for the better. We repeat patterns because when we go through a painful event at a young age – most significantly between the age of 0 and 6 – we then go onto living life from this memory, and that which we have gathered which appears to make logical sense.

Let me tell you something profound about the concept of memory. You tend to be driven right now by the things that happened to you in the early stages of your life.

But what if you could completely stop this programmed story to start a new recording – a new way of life? The universe listens to absolutely everything you think about. It responds to all thoughts and words; that which you think about becomes the frequency in which you vibrate at. Whatever you think about becomes your reality.

Soul Communication

❖ What ideas do you choose, consciously or otherwise?
❖ Is your story shaped around fear or unconditional love?
❖ Is your story shaped around sadness or joy?
❖ Is your bank account shaped around wealth or scarcity?

Whatever thoughts you choose, no matter what your mind focuses on, it will reflect and manifest externally. Since psychological coding happens from such a young age, the rebirthing process requires a gentle, kind, and loving approach to re-programming. We must hold focus around precisely what we would like to experience in life and grieve over the past experiences that have had a hold over us, before letting them go.

I am not here to say that everyone must wake up, right here, right now. I am supporting the idea that anyone who would like to recreate their life, must recognise the steady and loving process that must be applied to rebirth. After all, anything that aligns with the natural laws of the universe cannot be forced. Everything unfolds in divine timing. Everyone is on their own individual journey, and some may stay programmed their entire life. Is that wrong? Not at all. We all choose our lessons and we are all walking very subjective paths. We must allow everything to unfold naturally, rather than forcing an awakening.

Rebirthing the soul is an ongoing journey of evolution. It has no beginning or end. The first time I went through my rebirthing process was because I believed in the darkness of my thoughts. I gave my power away to past pain, playing out the role of a victim. I wanted to find meaning in the painful story that I was playing over and over, but without realising that this was all I was focusing on, the universe enhanced my story and suddenly, the dark depths of hell became my reality. I was stuck in my past and needed to transcend with love.

Do we have to go through suffering to wake up and make a change? Well, it sounds rather strange, but this experience was exactly what I needed to go through to wake up to the truth and the callings of my divine soul. The universe is neither blessing nor punishing us – it is simply responding to the vibration that we emit. It is beneficial to know that gratitude is the highest vibration in the entire universe. Send out gratitude and great things will return.

Fearful belief systems are quite possibly the greatest illusion that has rippled throughout the universal mind in human history. But if we look at our situations through the eyes of fear, then we are going to become even more clogged up with the garbage of our wounds. We must purge the illusion, and through this purge, we can begin to feel safe and whole again. We are safe on this earth and the changes that we go through; it is our home.

Sometimes I feel the need to give thanks to the great force of Mother Nature, bringing about the current global crisis. It has been the most significant, most unexpected gift that my soul has ever encountered. Let me tell you exactly why.

Firstly, it has stripped away everything from me that I falsely believed I needed, to be complete in this time and space. That stripping away has guided me to the point of surrender which I had so painfully resisted in the past. This situation has left me with what truly matters. Finally, I have come to discover the simplicity of what I require to be whole in this lifetime.

Well thank goodness this has happened. Thank goodness we are being shown 'reality' and the sickness that is created from playing it small and giving ourselves away to nothing but a system of slavery. Thank goodness millions have lost their jobs because this is a turning point for strength, courage, compassion and love to be born. People have now discovered their true calling instead of working their ass off for something that is not in alignment with the soul.

I sit here writing this book and finally sharing my story that I had avoided for so long. I sit here writing this book to finally help others transcend their fears into the greatest of light, creativity and gifts.

I have had to grieve and heal the parts of me that never genuinely believed in myself. That my voice should not be heard. That my story was not necessary. That mental illness, spiritual emergence, rebirth or whatever you would like to call it is a taboo topic.

I was riding horses from the age of ten because I was born to communicate with nature. I graduated with a Bachelor of Arts in Professional Writing because I was born to be a communicator. I fulfilled the role of a copywriter, busting my ass off for so many companies because I was born to learn self-worth so I could finally do something for myself. I fulfilled the role of an equine groom because I was born to learn the language of the soul. It does not matter whether I am writing or riding, what matters is that I am shining my light.

I am profoundly grateful for this crisis, teaching me that everything I once experienced served a higher purpose bringing me to this very moment. It is this very moment in which I have surrendered to the truth of my calling, which is to align with the frequency of love through always being in the heart. To feel into every emotion and see it as a gift. To do something for myself, instead of always doing everything for everyone else. To be in alignment with what anchors me into my heart, never giving in to any fear that surrounds me. To honor and cherish the love I was gifted by my father's side of the family. To be in a state of complete gratitude, and never needing to run away from who I truly am. To know that I will never need to take a substance to alter my mind again, for it is whole and it is healed. To simply trust in my intuitive guidance of the divine feminine. To let do this work and then let go of it, for I am no longer attached to past experiences, where I felt separated into right vs wrong. To choose wholeness.

CHAPTER 11

INTEGRATION

*"Wisdom is everywhere, waiting for you
to tap into its universal magic."*

I often cross paths with people who talk about the concept of how the earth is always upgrading its codes and energy, which is attempting to align with the 5th dimension. The truth is that the 5th dimension (a state of unconditionally loving consciousness) is *already* within us. I will talk more about the 5th dimension when we enter the 12th house of Pisces as the fish is symbolic of the spiritual dimension, as well as the concept of duality.

Ancient wisdom is the birth-right of our infinite soul. All we must do is tap into it. Tapping into this gift requires two processes to journey through.

1. Psychologically dying to all limiting belief systems that have driven your entire existence and no longer serve you.
2. Reprogramming your unconscious mind with the life that reflects heaven on earth for you.

Since heaven on earth is not a place, but rather, a state of consciousness, we must wake up to seeing what is unfolding within our reality. The reality you see right now is a manifestation of the exact thoughts that are an endless record playing over in your subconscious mind.

Soul Communication

- ❖ Do you like where you live?
- ❖ Do you like the job you are in?
- ❖ Do you like your relationships?

Olivia Blakey

Everything you choose is serving the goal for you to come into complete alignment with your soul's calling, whether you are aware of it or not.

You must get to the root cause of why you need to heal, and see through the pain trauma with the eyes of love. Know that it is not your fault that you were given your trauma, but it is your responsibility to heal it. Without reaching this and healing it, you will in fact 'escape' the current situation only to find yourself in the same position. The chances are that you picked up a belief system through a traumatic experience in the early stages of your life, attaching meaning to this trauma, and making sense of the outer world through this perception. The opinion has become your story, and it is playing over and over. So instead, see all of your healing and manifestations through the eyes of love and forgiveness for any past experiences. See the present moment as a gift, providing you great opportunities. Embody the energetic vibration that you would love to be. Keep it simple and keep it based on the joys and abundance of life.

The exciting news is that every single moment is a beautiful opportunity to evolve, and moments of dislike are the very things that prompt us to heal and improve. They are here to awaken you to see the divinity of love in everyone and everything.

When you communicate on the level of the soul, you are operating in the 5th dimension of devotion. When you live, breathe and work from the 5th dimension, you are a boundless divine being and all your creations flourish. When you dedicate yourself to remembering the ancient wisdom of the language of the soul, you can truly connect with your billion-dollar inner guide and discover your most authentic self. You can align with the vibrational frequency of love, and watch this materialize into your physical world.

Have you ever participated in a cacao ceremony? This sacred earth medicine which derives from Peru, is often used in ecstatic dance and ritual, bringing communities together to celebrate life. Ceremonial cacao supported me on the journey of writing this book, opening my heart, so that the words can flow from a place of love. I am deeply grateful for integrating this ancient medicine into this soulful project.

While this book certainly highlights the lows of what was once a depressed soul, I would like to refer to these experiences and share what I have learned from it, as if it were a past life. I am genuinely appreciative for those lows, for they are the very reason I was able to be reborn. However, I must refer to this as the past because I am living a newfound way that is far more liberating and look forward to the exciting future that awaits. Greatness is already unfolding as I share these words.

When you are reborn, you cross boundaries. Your rebirth journey transcends logic, and while the ego would much prefer to make up more stories of fear to point the finger at others and protect itself, the truth is this. You are divine. You always have been divine and always will be.

Life is not happening to you – it is happening for you. When one's belief system focuses on the concept that life is a struggle and unfair, then that is what life shall bring. Life will bring you this experience because that is the story in which you have created in your mind. Those who experience extreme suffering may feel the constant need to attain more, always running away from what reality is providing them. We must keep moving forward on our journey through surrendering to the lessons that we are being taught by others. We must know that we do not always need to attain more because we already have everything within us.

Selfish, competitive, and narcissistic thinking can no longer survive when we tap into ancient wisdom. To flow with life, we must move with the cycles of Mother Nature; we must be like bamboo, bending without breaking, adapting to the rhythms of nature. When we resist the rhythms of nature, we resist life. Our ancient wisdom from our ancestor's teachings is the catalyst for remembering unity.

Before I take you further into this journey, I must highlight one of the most important themes in this book. Blame is not the answer. Blaming others or blaming yourself does not solve anything. Every step in the process of awakening requires unconditional love and an approach that is free of judgement.

Soul Communication

- ❖ What ancient wisdom do you need to embody into your life?
- ❖ What story is handed down to you from your ancestors?
- ❖ How can you transform the negative stories and personify the positive?

Your soul is boundless – it cannot possibly resonate with the constraints of life since it only knows limitless abundance. You can achieve a connection with the playfulness of your soul through daily practice of getting out of limited ways of thinking and into the unconditionally loving heart space.

Heart-based activity includes meditation, barefoot walking in nature, gratitude journaling, horse riding, swimming, dancing, singing, creating and expressing yourself in many other healthy ways. Know that whatever lights up your soul is heart-based activity, and there is no right or wrong journey.

Always remember that the point is not so much about what you are doing, but rather, how you embrace it with presence. When we move into our heart through the things we love, we can ultimately shift our energy field into a whole new dimension. This type of shift calls for immense healing, insight and is the centre of manifesting with caring intention.

Since your soul is boundless, it would be a lost moment of magic if you did not check in with your inner guru each day. Your inner guide is your billion-dollar navigator, driving you towards more of what you need, so that you can do great things for yourself, others and the planet.

This is not about mastering your life the exact moment you check-in with your internal world, but rather, it is a sacred ritual that can empower you to truly nourish the light within. It is about allowing yourself to be in flow with the callings of your soul every single day. It is an ever-evolving, ever-expanding journey. And when we take the time to go within and remember that we are stars wrapped in skin, then the internal world of love, peace and harmony become a vibrational match in our outer circumstances.

Soul Communication

❖ How can you learn to understand the bigger picture?
❖ How can you be comfortable in accepting all that is and be inspired to make changes where they may be needed?
❖ How can you trust that what you seek is seeking you?

I believe that every experience serves a higher purpose. I believe that through the pain, you will be guided to more superior forms of love. My past addictions were the very thing that taught me to form self-control. I believe that those who struggle with low self-esteem are being guided to become more aligned with confidence. One cannot exist without the other, for we live in a dualistic world that is kept in divine order through the laws of nature. We are here to learn from the shadows and we certainly can transcend them.

If in doubt, do not ever stop reminding yourself that you are a boundless being and that you can be propelled forward from *any* setback. Your setbacks are the very reason for your evolution.

Sit with your fear long enough, and it will be transformed into an energy of love, through accepting and releasing. Try not to think too much about why you feel something, but instead tap into your heart space. This is the frequency of Mother Earth, our beautiful home. Sit in your darkness long enough, and you will find the light. As we let go of the reins of resistance that we attempt to control outside ourselves and instead, sink into our hearts, the world around us begins to alter dramatically.

Wayne Dyer's book, 'The Power of Intention,' states, *"Change the way you look at things and the things you look at will change."* This so beautifully exemplifies the power of soul work and how we must adjust our inner world if we desire to change our outer world.

To find yourself – really, truly, authentically find the most unique parts of yourself – you first must lose yourself. You must lose every part of yourself that is locked in limitation which has been projected onto you from your past experiences. You must release all the garbage with loving forgiveness, knowing it was just a lesson and standing in the truth of seeing that it no longer serves you. You must be willing to see past the smoky mirrors because they are blocking you from the infinite abundance of your soul.

Soul Communication

I am on a journey to rebuilding my most authentic truth. I am recreating my purest most unique sense of self, and I allow myself to love every single moment of it. I let go of the old and open space for the new. I release old limiting ways of thinking, so that I can become aligned with my soul's calling. I am a divine being on a journey to ever-evolving expansion. May all those who are trapped by the limitations of what they once thought they were defined as, find the power and strength to be reborn. Authentically. Lovingly. Abundantly. So be it!

CHAPTER 12

THE 3RD SOUL COMMUNICATION

*"Forgiveness is the most profound journey
that is born from the soul."*

Stand in front of a mirror and look into the universal window of your eyes. Take a few moments to stare into them. Take note of the colour of your eye. Do your eyes feel light? Soft? Heavy? Dull?

Stay here and allow yourself to fully absorb the truthful emotions that your eyes reflect. Be prepared for some strong emotions to rise to the surface.

Once you have connected with your soul, repeat the following affirmations whilst continuing to look into your eyes through the mirror.

In this deep place of forgiveness, allow any emotions to come through and be released.

Affirm: *"I am here to learn lessons and evolve. My soul is perfect. I am complete."*

Affirm: *"All my choices have served a greater purpose. I choose to bring forward wisdom, love and joy as I forgive and free myself from all past limitations."*

Affirm: *"I forgive you. I forgive you. I forgive you. I freely forgive you with all of my heart."*

Repeat as many times as necessary. The longer time you spend in this forgiveness ritual, the deeper you will connect with your soul's purity. The deeper you connect with the divinity and unconditional love of your soul, the more you will expand and open to receive your most authentic alignment. You enter the quest for thriving in all areas of life.

CHAPTER 13

THE CRAB

"I accept that I sometimes feel all emotions – from fear to love. Both ends of the spectrum are sacred, teaching and guiding me to my wholeness."

Sign: Cancer
Ruler: The Moon
Element: Water
Season: Summer
Colour: White
Stone: Moonstone
Light elements: Creative, Intuitive, Feminine, Gentle, Unity
Shadow elements: Lunatic, Withdrawn, Separated, Needy, Chaotic

The 4th house is symbolic of the mother energy. Not only is this house a reflection of our home – the great Mother Earth – it is also a reflection of the womb in which all life is created. When we journey through the 4th house of Cancer we are taken through the realm of the feminine dimension. The feminine dimension speaks of all things related to emotion.

This is a place where emotions create chaos if they have been suppressed. The crab lives inside a shell, which is essentially its home, and you will see that the crab retreats inwards to its shell, hiding when feeling threatened or fearful. This is a beautiful metaphor for what humanity goes through when they become suppressed by their own fears. We must learn to express healthily, feeling all the emotional spectrum knowing that it is safe to do so.

If we are overthinking and overdoing, stuck in the dimension of the masculine, then we have lost all connection to the creative, intuitive, gentle, and unified aspects of the light that is born from the feminine dimension. It is said that the absence of the feminine equals addiction. Is there any wonder we are living on a timeline that is consumed by addiction? The current state of the world is being called to become more aligned and in tune between the balance of both masculine and feminine. The good news is that we are on the way to a more balanced state of energy between the feminine and masculine energies. We are on our way to union.

What does this mean? It means knowing when to move forward, do the work and act, as well as knowing when to slow down, go within and simply be. That is the power of living in balance between both dimensions.

Soul Communication

❖ What elements of the crab's light are reflected in your life?

❖ What elements of the crab's shadow are reflected in your life?

❖ Are you healthy in your expression of all emotion or are you suppressing out of fear of being seen and heard?

❖ How is your soul calling you to live more aligned with the feminine dimension?

❖ Are you in balance between the feminine and masculine concepts of life?

CHAPTER 14

THE FEMININE DIMENSION

"I embody the positive elements of divine feminine nature."

Without the light elements of the feminine dimension, the masculine dimension is simply unable to go through the process of healing. The feminine dimension brings about qualities that enable the masculine to feel nurtured and held by her intuitive and flowing rhythm. Positive attributes of the feminine dimension include:

- Sensitive
- Vulnerable
- Creative
- Ability to receive
- Good at listening
- Trusting
- Soft
- Intuitive
- Connected
- Emotionally communicative
- Expressive
- Sensual

When a woman is stuck in the shadows of the feminine dimension, it often means that she is completely disconnected from her wonderful emotional center of energy, the gift of feeling and embodying deep love. If this is the case, this can mean that she runs the risk of feeling suppressed and lacking her creative flow towards life and all its greatness. This can mean that they feel suppressed and lack their creative flow towards life and all its greatness. The shadow elements of the feminine dimension often manifest when someone is disconnected from their emotional nature and stuck in their logical thinking patterns. These types of people cannot flow with life, which often causes tension and feelings of being stuck and restricted to the pains of trying to make it in a solely masculine world. The shadow elements of the feminine dimension include:

- Chaos
- Withdrawn
- Emotionally unstable
- Careless
- Crazy
- Co-dependent
- Inconsiderate
- Reckless
- Stuck
- Resisting
- Lacking compassion
- All giving or all taking
- Extremist
- Self-centred

The purpose of the feminine dimension is to nurture, sustain, create, flow, heal and tap into all intuitive mystery. It is a magical dimension that feels instead of relying on facts and thinking. This feminine dimension is present to bring about the deepest of love that nurtures the masculine aspect. Just like a mother nurtures her baby, the feminine element is wise in compassion, nurturing all of life, internally and externally. You are a free-flowing, creative, nourishing, healing and mystical expression of the Divine Feminine, so embrace exactly that.

The feminine dimension is an element that is present in both women and men, just like the masculine dimension is an element that is present in men as well as women. In ancient Indian traditions, the feminine aspect is known to be divine cosmic energy that represents dynamic forces that move through the universe – this force is known as Shakti.

Shakti is responsible for creation and is the agent of change, often manifested to destroy dark forces and restore balance. This vital cosmic force in which all men and women have access to, is the power center in which one can transcend old ways into new.

Shakti is working through us in every moment – it is the magic of life that moves through the womb of humanity. It makes fingernails grow and hearts beat, navigates souls from the astral to the earth realm, and births some of the greatest music, arts and other creative projects in the world.

In any moment, you can call upon your inner Shakti energy to access her power and fertility. This power and fertility are known throughout history to be the energy that is born from transcending fearful troubles into the restoration of love. One is born through the fire of destroying old and birthing anew.

This feminine energy, however, is not a type of power in which the ego construct should abuse. Shakti sees beyond 'the self' sourcing the life energy force from unity consciousness. Those who understand this energy will, therefore, understand that Shakti stands for oneness deriving from heart-based leadership. It is consequently impossible to utilise the feminine dimension for intentions of greed or self-interest, but rather work with Shakti to create a change that serves the greater sense of all, for both humanity and the earth.

The feminine dimension speaks of community. The creative waters of this deeply dreamy and imaginative flow is what creates worlds that destroy old ways of suffering through simply striving to make it alone, in a hierarchical structure. Shakti is far from that – Shakti says, instead of me making it at the cost of your suffering or vice versa, you and I both make it, together.

The feminine dimension, at its empowered and conscious level, rejoices in the elements of love, compassion, unity, creativity, flow, nourishment, trust and surrender. When one is disempowered, the unconscious desires to be driven by the feminine, which is led by submission, neediness, victimhood, and manipulation. These energies have long been buried in the depths of the human psyche through the patriarchal structures of learning to 'make it' in a hierarchical society. This darkness within our being has been trapped for too long, forming the shadow parts of oneself, that the ego has simply denied its existence.

Through decades upon decades of suppression, we have now reached a time where archetypes of the feminine that rise to the surface have become classed as madness. Since we are so unfamiliar with integrating these parts into our daily life, we must learn to acknowledge them rather than reject, deny and resist them.

Depression and other mental illnesses have been witnessed through the eyes of fear, with the modern ways of western society turning a blind eye to this psychological disturbance. We are confronted with something of foreign lands and rather than seeking the wisdom that is locked in the depth of what is trying to emerge, we put a band-aid over the problem itself. We numb out the intense emotion in which the feminine dimension brings forth, medicating with all sorts of substances so that we simply cannot feel and transcend the energy from suffering, to love.

It was only a few years ago (when I transitioned into my late twenties) in which I discovered that if I was to hold onto the resentment towards the pain and suffering that had emerged in my life, that I would be no different to operating with fear-based thinking.

When we release all ideas around who is to blame and stop pointing the finger, we can be truly liberated from the past, allowing us to flow into a future in which a new story is born.

The masculine dimension needs forgiveness now more than ever. It is the role of the feminine energy to perform this. Not only so that we can enter a new level of consciousness by journeying to the well of worlds to cleanse the collective soul of humanity – but simply because – we need him just as much as we need to enter the gateway to the feminine dimension.

Gaia is the mother goddess who presided over the earth. The ancestral mother of life, she by all accounts, resides on the planet, offering a home and nourishment to all her children. Living on through many ancient civilisations, Gaia is revered as the mother source of energy that both nurtures and gives life to the very existence that we are part of here today on this beautiful planet. It is said that Gaia was born from the emptiness in the chaos that created the entire universe. Symbolic of the land, trees, and fruits, she is depicted in art as a voluptuous maternal figure – a woman's body that is simply unable to divide herself from the earth.

We have reached a time in history where humanity is being asked to remember the concepts of Gaia and how it is in our nature to be at one with the feminine, enabling ourselves to be in balance between giving and receiving. To remember, we must burn that which no longer serves and rise like a phoenix from the purity of these ashes.

It is not our duty to 'save' the planet. The great Mother Earth has strength and resilience that is more powerful than we will ever be able to comprehend – she will always find a way to renew herself. We however must save ourselves. When we've finally purged, released, and healed the wounds that have clogged up our psyche, driving us to act out in selfish and fearful ways, humanity will then be able to respect and appreciate the sacredness of life, treating ourselves and others with unconditional love and compassion.

Waiting to be born, the new paradigm is divine union, wholeness and joy between humanity, which has been disconnected by fear for many centuries. It is no longer a time of patriarchy or matriarchy – but instead – the masculine and feminine in perfect harmony, creating new earth consciousness, together.

I write this book not just because I have been through my journey into the underworld, but because I believe there is a call to rise to new ways of understanding the feminine. The irony of mental illness on this planet is that it has been masked with a sense of weakness and often classed as 'taboo'.

It takes a lot of breakthroughs in such a paradigm in which humanity has become caught up in. It is as if we are in this trance of pushing to race against time, unconsciously driven by the mental patterns that reinforce the idea of kindness being weakness and surrender being disempowering. The opposite is exact.

Growing up in a large family was one of the many reasons why I was still striving for an individualised path at the age of twenty-five. I am not saying that individuation is unnecessary – humans need to follow the way that is most aligned for themselves.

However, in times of struggle, fear, and suffering, it is vital now more than ever for the one who attempts to make it alone, to reach out for support in all areas possible. This can be family, friends, mentors, councillors, healers and other forms of community. It can be as simple as picking up the phone to tell someone that you simply do not feel like yourself and need some help to become more aligned with the available support.

CHAPTER 15

CONSCIOUS CREATION

"The challenge in life is not to honour the white wolf, and avoid the black wolf, but to merge the two and become the grey. The grey wolf that lives both truths."

Wholeness is not about denying the mistakes, setbacks, and darkness. It is about taking the wisdom from these experiences, owning them, and integrating them into our achievements, opportunity and light.

The ego is focused on the things we believe that we are, and the shadow is focused on the things we believe that we are not. But the truth is that we are everything.

When we encompass both mindfulness and acceptance through integrating the ego and shadow elements of ourselves, we are in total harmony. So, how can we achieve wholeness through owning all parts of ourselves – light and darkness?

Wholeness is being both sides of the coin. It is the assimilation of purity from the white wolf and the wisdom from the black wolf. Wholeness is unremittingly coming from a place of knowing. Knowing that each end of the scale of emotion serves its purpose.

Since so many of us have been taught to deny emotions from a young age, there are often certain aspects of ourselves that are suppressed, rejected and denied because we do not permit ourselves to feel what we believe to be wrong. For example, feeling sad can often be perceived as a negative emotion, but this is certainly something that needs to be felt when someone close to us dies. We must grieve over these experiences to become stronger, resilient and wiser through the journey of the soul.

Dis-ease is the spiritual starvation of the soul.

By denying certain emotions and honouring others, we create disconnection from the essence of humanity. Given that the patriarchy has deemed certain emotions 'taboo' and encouraged one to close off from their nature, it's no surprise we've created a box in the backroom of the psyche that we would rather not open the door to. It is no surprise that the rate of suicide is increasing, and we are unable to understand mental health – how can we understand something if we are pushing it away with shame and fear. This must change if we are to return to our true nature of being a wholesome human.

The box in the backroom contains all the frequencies that the ego denies. This box in the back room has been closed shut for decades through masking with immense distraction outside of ourselves.

But there can only be so much numbing, silencing, and shutting down of these energies. Since they are a part of nature, it can only be a matter of time before the shadow strikes out. Inauthenticity cannot survive and if there is anything that knows this truth, it is your soul.

Rather than keeping that box of unwanted beliefs in the backroom and denying ownership, the feminine within is asking to take a step back and let the shadow elements be seen, and more importantly, heard. She is asking for love, forgiveness, acceptance, and most importantly, integration and complete ownership of these energies.

Perhaps when we return to the balance of our internal compass, the soul can begin its work, integrating both the black and white wolves. And when the grey wolf emerges, then the creative self-expression can flow and we can truly become aligned with the callings of the infinite soul, holding hands with the universe.

Soul Communication

- ❖ Are you in touch with your inner wolves?
- ❖ How balanced are they?
- ❖ Are both your black and white wolf seen and heard?
- ❖ How can your soul integrate the two so that you can return to your real and raw humanness?
- ❖ What gifts can you bring to the world if you journey into both the elements of day and night?

If you would like to delve deeper into the underworld of shadow and truly befriend your black wolf, you can learn more by exploring the theories and works of Carl Jung.

The journey to inner freedom begins when we shine our light on all parts of ourselves, expressing every colour of our emotions. The moment things feel wrong is the moment we attempt to swim upstream, resisting the flow of life and its ever-changing frequency. We must be willing to feel everything if we are ready to return to wholeness.

Only when we hold the space to truly communicate with our soul will we connect to the wellbeing and power that lives within self-expression.

So, while Mother Earth probes us to rewire our spiritual core, let's take a second to forgive ourselves for any of the soul-destroying moments that once controlled us, and all of the people in our lives who are caught up in chaos and disconnect. We can only commence on this journey with a sense of compassion for oneself.

Self-healing and soul retrieval begin with a heart that is open to love. It does not matter how used or abused, rejected, or denied, lost, or confused you once felt, every moment is offering you love to be received.

So be open to it.

Love yourself and love every part of yourself! Your trauma, your mistakes, your failure, and your knockbacks. Your success, your beauty, your bravery and your curiosity.

Soul Communication

I am connected to every part of my soul. I am connected to every part of my soul's perfection and wholeness. I trust in the guidance my soul brings me, surrendering to the precision of where it will lead me. In trusting this guidance, I open myself up to immeasurable opportunity, strength, and support. I speak my authenticity into existence. May all those who are battling fear and doubt on their path find comfort in allowing their soul's promptings to be received and use the power of soul communication to co-create their best life. So be it!

Your soul already knows that everything you have, want and need is already inside of you.

We have all been there, attempting to escape the body and free the mind because our outer circumstances can often seem like a reality that we would rather not be a part of. But in the act of unhealthy escapism through short term fixes, we create so much more darkness and uncertainty in our lives, never really feeling grounded or connected to the earth.

If we cannot accept our outer circumstances with love then the reality is that we cannot accept ourselves, because we are the ones who create everything. The circumstances we do not really like are the things we have asked for to learn and grow through. We must learn to be with each experience and love where we are at before we can move forward and experience something new. If we choose to hate on our circumstances then perhaps, we will remain locked in them forever. Perhaps therefore so many people experience the same repetitive patterns over and over as they are choosing the same lesson over and over and never really learning from it.

For myself, co-dependent relationships once held me back from standing strong in the centre of empowerment. I often felt like I could not do great things unless I had the approval of others. And this is not uncommon for many. So many are afraid to shine bright in their magnitude due to decades upon decades of societal conditioning that has silenced the voices of those who have important messages that need to be heard.

Not only has this left a wound in the psyche, it has left both men and women unsure of themselves and disconnected from one another. The truth is there is no use in fighting for equality or blaming and shaming the opposite gender – we must unite in wholeness because we have so much to learn from one another. We are far more powerful when the masculine and feminine are in holy union.

Whatever is buried within the shadow elements of the self, know that the shadow is here to teach the power of profound love that is born through integrating all parts of the self. Know that the shadow is the part of ourselves asking for courage to dig deeper. Dig deeper so that we can, once and for all, stand authentically in our wholeness. When we own all parts of ourselves, we return to a state of harmony, and better still, we can recover the parts of ourselves that we once repressed, rejected, or denied. Often, these are the parts of ourselves that enable us to uncover our greatest gifts.

When dealing with the shadow, a lot of shame and guilt can rise to the surface, triggering the inner critic since these are the parts that we often judge in others, because we deny them within ourselves. We must put aside all judgment if we are to traverse the world of integration. We need to be gentle on the rawest parts of ourselves. We must nurture these parts of ourselves. We should embody forgiveness, not only for ourselves, but for others.

Mother Nature is the source of all creation. She is our home. She is our foundation. She is our most authentic reflection of who we are at our deepest core. When our inner world is denied, suppressed, or rejected, the soul's light fades and that is when it calls for a deep need to return to its natural state, where you will feel more aligned; feel at home with yourself.

I believe that depression is your soul forcing you to stop what you are doing. I believe that depression is your soul prompting you to take deep rest.

Here and now, in this deep resting space your soul can finally ask you to look within – look deeply at your emotions and enter a space of introspection. Here is where you can reflect in the stillness to discover the things that need eliminating from your life so that you can live in a more healthy, loving, joyful and abundant time and space within the universe. Perhaps depression is your soul asking you to stop, release the garbage and recreate yourself. Perhaps depression is your soul attempting to go through the rebirth process.

If society perceived depression as a profoundly transforming moment of pure rest, we would be living a completely different way of life. We would be honouring our mind, body and soul in this resting space. We would take the time to listen to what is required since we are all too often distracted by the chaos. During moments like depression, we are not only being asked to hear the prayers of the soul, we are being asked to be reborn, so that we can become aligned with them.

I believe your soul is here to show you how resistant you can be, and this resistance is unnecessary. I believe your soul is here to remind you what truly matters to you and guide you towards these things in life. I believe your soul is here to assist you in letting go of the garbage you carry and choosing to align with the newness of everything you deserve.

So, if at any given moment on your journey of the soul you cease to remember why you have been forced into a place of looking at your most painful wounds – then remember this – your soul is calling to be reborn.

CHAPTER 16

THE 4ᵀᴴ SOUL COMMUNICATION

"I am the divine creator of my own reality."

Write some statements that light you up, so that you can practice becoming intentionally focused on anchoring the infinite abundance of your soul into your reality. Check out some of my examples before you create your own.

"I am an ever-changing limitless being and I can always choose the highest vibrational thoughts to improve my mindset."

Olivia Blakey

"All of my experiences, lessons, and choices are perfect, and my soul is here to teach me this."

"I surrender to the perfection of my transformation and enjoy the process."

"It is safe to change and become the person I am ready to be because it will bring me more abundance, love, health, creativity, and freedom."

"I am guided by a high vibration of love and I choose to manifest this from my inner world into my outer world."

_____

_____

_____

_____

Write a letter to your inner critic, from your higher-self, highlighting your awareness and the reminder of what shapes your wholeness and humanity – both the dark and the light. Allow your emotions to flow so that your shadow can truly emerge from the stirring waters of your inner ocean, complete in all its expression.

Remember that your shadows are the fragmented parts of yourself that are attempting to be integrated and these parts of you give rise to some of the most profound creative gifts that can guide you to living a more abundant life, when recognised. It is important to never reject parts of ourselves that we do not like, but rather, let them be seen and heard so that we can transcend them into more love and light. Here is an example letter.

Dear inner-critic,

Thank you for always being there, ready to protect me. Thank you for aiming to maintain a state of perfection, however, I am here to remind you that I am already enough – my soul confirms that I am already perfectly divine.

I want to give thanks to the copious amounts of drugs, alcohol, and unhealthy foods I once consumed, for this has taught me to listen to my emotions rather than shutting them out and silencing my sensitivity. My soul is infinitely abundant and each of my emotions are worth feeling. Every destructive choice happened because I was hurting and wanted to remain numb, but now I am choosing love. I choose to feel every emotion because that is what makes me human – that is what helps me to deliver some of the most powerful work as a creative writer who is great at shaping narratives and storytelling.

I want to thank the dark hole of doubt that once lived inside of me. I was often trapped in a dark tunnel within my mind feeling like I wanted to escape the curse that I believed came with being a sensitive soul. I give thanks to this experience as it acts as a reminder of never wanting to return to such destructive ways ever again. I would rather feel the entire spectrum of emotion and move forward into love, joy and abundance which is what I deserve. These experiences served a purpose since everything is just a lesson. No longer do I need to learn this lesson. I move forward into my creativity and wholeness, integrating all parts of myself that were once fragmented.

With unconditional love, Olivia

Now write your letter:

_____

_____

_____

_____

_____

_____

_____

_____

_____

_____

_____

_____

_____

_____

_____

_____

CHAPTER 17

THE LION

"I will always be dedicated to love, play and creativity."

Sign: Leo
Ruler: The Sun
Element: Fire
Season: Summer
Colour: Gold
Stone: Citrine
Light elements: Heart-centred, Influential, Active, Open, Playful
Shadow elements: Fiery, Angry, Immature, Multifaceted, Self-centred

When we journey through the 5th house of the lion we are brought to the very centre of our hearts. In this wonderful space that is connected to the love, purity, and innocence of the inner child, we are truly connected to our soul's need to be expressive, creative and embrace the power of play.

This is the house where we are creators in the making and when we can truly manifest from a space of love. When we shift out of mind and into heart, we can begin to learn that life does not always have to be 'doing' for the pure reason that it will bring an outcome. Rather, we can dance, sing, play, paint, write and create for the sheer fun of it.

This heart space calls for the need to be open to receiving from the universe. If we are open to receiving, then we can become the creators of our most authentic path. However, those who are closed off from the mission of their soul will find themselves stuck in the shadows being called to transmute the fire that continues to burn.

Living in the shadows of the lion is often reflected by anger. This anger can leave one stuck in a place of pain if they are unable to transcend their wounds and fears into the love and compassion that is required for rising and rebirthing the soul.

Olivia Blakey

Soul Communication

- ❖ What elements of the lion's light are reflected in your life?
- ❖ What elements of the lion's shadow are reflected in your life?
- ❖ How can you use your fire to transcend your fears to love?
- ❖ Where in your life are you being called to be more creative and playful, living from the heart?

Leo energy is linked to the Lion's Gate portal which happens every August. The energy for this fire and passion is particularly at its most potent on 08/08. When we enter the time and space of Lion's Gate portal, we are being called to elevate higher and birth all our creations from spirit into matter.

I would like to shout out to all the Leo's friends in my life. Many of them are creative souls who have always encouraged me to fulfil my career as a writer.

CHAPTER 18

THE HEART DIMENSION

"Let your soul be your billion-dollar inner guide. Let your mind be the faithful servant and let your body be the trusted communicator."

The heart chakra opens when the mind, body and soul are in harmonious rhythm.

When the mind, body and soul work together, they can each bring forward unique gifts to create a rhythmic flow of harmony. It is far too common for humanity to be in a battle between these three elements. The mind says, "get to work!" and the body says, "time to rest!" while the soul is already complete within the infinite universe of its current time and space.

Anyone who has sat in the saddle before will know how important it is to give and take when handling a horse that is connected to the reins. Hold on too hard, pulling at the horse's mouth and you will create an unstoppable fight. But if you are to gently pull back for just a brief moment, then release the grip, you will discover that the horse knows its place and through the rhythm of contact and release, the horse will happily work with you.

The horse and rider are a beautiful symbol of how we too, can master the association between the mind, body, and soul. We must attain an essence of balance, being considerate about the multidimensional elements of ourselves and how they must be integrated with love.

Humans have discovered the incredible power of the mind, for it is just as easy to destroy our outer circumstances as it is to create them. We can also spend too much time in the deep-set of the mind, losing touch with the body and all its messages from the emotional field. Given that the patriarchy taught us to deny our intuitive haunches, it is no surprise that many have disconnected from the gifts that come with emotion.

The body is calling for us to tune into the way we feel, now more than ever. The body holds both trauma and wisdom that has been passed down from our ancestors. Perhaps we can take a profound look into the intelligence of the body. Perhaps all the answers have always been here ready for us to utilise.

When we rely on the body's impulses and response to situations, we fuel ourselves with trust. To be your own beloved, parent, teacher, and guide, you must work on strengthening that intuitive muscle each day. As the communicator, the body can assist the soul in its journey of evolution. But first, you must learn to trust and believe in your intuition.

Thousands of years ago, women and men were tortured, hung, burnt, and killed for sharing their healing gifts with others. Whether we are consciously aware of it or not, we are on a quest to return to our body's natural rhythms because that is where we shall find our greatest gifts. We require a full connection between the emotions and the callings of the soul, to navigate our way through life with wisdom and flow. This trauma that dates back for thousands of years has left a wound in the collective psyche.

It is in our blood, bones, and DNA to be our own healers. It is natural to be working with plants, animals, elements, and the cycles. This connection between humans and Mother Earth has been lost and so we have embarked on a journey that is cleansing the collective soul. We have been forced to see our truth. Rebirth that is seen through the eyes of western medicine certainly reflects a great call for doing all that we can, to truly be in wholeness between mind, body and soul. Amazonian medicine and alternative modalities have been used for aeons of time to gain huge insight into the process of transcending darkness to light.

During my journey of working with Rapé, Kambo and Sananga, I discovered my need to flow with life rather than hold onto the past in a state of fear. These Amazonian medicines taught me that I was the only one who was holding myself back – when I live in a state of fear, I put barriers in the way of manifesting my best life. Working with this natural medicine opened doors in my heart, enabling me to see through the eyes of love.

This is valid for all of us, for fear lives in the collective consciousness. We must consciously choose to tap into love every single day, focusing on joy, abundance and prosperity in this present moment. We must surrender and free ourselves from the past, for it no longer exists. We must hold the vision of our future in our hearts, allowing ourselves to be guided to our greatest callings of the soul each day. We must take action to manifest the things that serve our highest good. We must practice what we preach. And most of all, we must surrender in trusting that everything is always unfolding in divine, perfect harmony.

Fear is the cause of dis-ease as well as stress and anxiety. If we are to declutter the mind, body and soul, we require a significant amount of compassion, forgiveness and love for ourselves.

To work with the inner rhythms of one's emotions is to fully encompass all that you are, without resistance. As we strive to be whole in our humanness, allowing the mind to speak love into existence, we carry a safe place for the full expression of the all-loving soul. This way, men can feel comfortable in all their birth-right to vulnerabilities and softness. Women can discover that the only way to heal the next generation, is by first healing themselves.

You see, the wounds are always waiting. Patiently. Waiting patiently to be allowed to fully rise to the surface. We must take the time to treat our emotional and mental wounds with the love and care that they need to heal.

And as we honour these internal conflicts, holding space, allowing the body to communicate its needs and truths, our soul can begin to show us unfolding bliss of what we so deeply need and deserve in this lifetime.

CHAPTER 19

THE POWER OF PLAY

*"I rejoice in the creative arts, allowing my energy
to be channelled into pure positivity."*

In Hinduism, Lila is a reference that is connected to the association of non-duality. Within non-dualism, Lila is a way of describing all existence, including the entire universe, as the outcome of play that is created by the divine.

When one is in a state of play, they are not so much chained to the game of life, but rather seeing through the eyes of the heart. They are soulfully connected to the innocence, purity, love and creativity of the inner child.

When we journey through the 5th house, we are beings of light in a state of creative play. Life that is created in the 4th house, through the womb of the feminine dimension, is then followed by living in a state of love. When we are journeying through the heart of the lion, we are being called to the power of play, just like every child does without questioning.

When you get some spare time, enjoy some playful moments. This comes in the form of:

- Cooking
- Baking
- Writing
- Painting
- Dancing
- Singing

There are many more ways to take part in play. You are standing in your light when you do all these things without expecting an outcome. You play just to simply enjoy life and all its beauty.

Soul Communication

- ❖ What is your favourite way to take time out?
- ❖ How often do you take time out for yourself to enjoy life?

CHAPTER 20

THE 5ᵀᴴ SOUL COMMUNICATION

"With every deep breath I sink into, I become more aligned."

Use some space clearing mist, a sage smudge or palo santo to clear the energy around you. Or, simply set the intention within your mind to clear the space with pure, loving energy.

Now, create your surroundings that most resonate with your soul. You can use flowers, a candle, incense, crystals, essential oils, photographs, lucky totems, and/or any other sacred items that help you to build and connect with your soul. There are no rules with this – use whatever you intuitively feel called to.

Now, take some time to yourself to be present in this quiet space. Sit with your legs crossed on the floor, using a cushion for comfort if needed.

Conscious breath-work is an extremely healing tool that allows one to reach the core of their inner being. Close your eyes and breathe for a few moments allowing each breath in to reach down past your lungs. Allow each breath to reach your stomach and beyond, into your hips. When we breathe into the solar plexus, we create an anchor between our own heart, and the heart of Mother Earth. Continue with this until achieving a state of both grounding and softness within your body and aura.

Now, place your hand on your heart.

Visualise a bright, golden light here. This light is the energetic blueprint of your soul. Your soul holds every answer here.

Ask your soul, *"What guidance do you have for me today?"* Remain here in this peaceful space, breathing into the question and connecting with your soul for as long as required.

Your soul responds in many ways. It may use visuals such as symbols, numbers, words, colours or animals. Trust whatever comes through.

Sometimes, your guidance can be received almost instantly. Sometimes, you may hear, feel, or see nothing at all. Know that you are always receiving exactly what you need to receive at that given moment. This exercise can be done each day to guide you towards taking the action that your soul is prompting.

> **"Mind, body and soul alignment creates**
> **powerful, intentional manifestation."**

My mindset needs to be focused on:

_____
_____
_____
_____

From making note of my thoughts I can use this information to create more:

_____
_____
_____
_____
_____
_____
_____
_____
_____
_____

My body is telling me to focus on:

_____
_____
_____
_____
_____
_____
_____
_____
_____

Olivia Blakey

From making note of my feelings I can use this information to create more of the things I love including:

_____

_____

_____

_____

_____

_____

_____

_____

My soul is guiding me to focus on:

_____

_____

_____

_____

_____

_____

_____

_____

In following such guidance, I can/will create:

_____

_____

_____

_____

_____

_____

_____

_____

_____

_____

Walking through the burning flames of all my fears makes me feel:

_____

_____

_____

_____

_____

_____

_____

_____

_____

_____

I resist opening to receive the new because I am afraid of:

_____

_____

_____

_____

_____

_____

Olivia Blakey

_____

_____

_____

_____

If I allow myself to release old patterns, I will be able to move forward and achieve:

_____

_____

_____

_____

_____

_____

_____

_____

The purest parts of myself that will always remain are:

_____

_____

_____

_____

_____

_____

_____

_____

Soul Communication

Across time and space, I choose to free myself from limitations. I choose to trust the process of purification. I choose to allow my old self to completely surrender within the burning flames, allowing my most authentic self to emerge and stand strong in truth. I am an infinite, powerful being. May all those who fear the ferocity of the burning flames find courage to walk through and destroy all that they are not. May all those who walk through the burning flames be guided to embodying their highest truth. So be it!

**"A new path is forged through the flames
that burn and release the old."**

Write a list of ten limiting beliefs that hold you back from living in alignment with your soul.

_____

_____

_____

_____

_____

_____

_____

_____

_____

_____

Now take a moment to tune into your centre. Whether it means meditating for twenty minutes or simply closing your eyes and taking three deep breaths into your heart.

Ask your higher self, *"How do these experiences no longer define me?"*

Then write a list of ten feelings that your heart most resonates with, for example, you may desire to achieve a stronger state of health, love, joy, creativity, inner peace, clarity or freedom. Write exactly why you would like to align with these feelings.

Next to each of these feelings that you desire to create more of. Write your intentions focusing on what action you will take to attract more of these vibrations into your life. Perhaps you will dedicate one day a week to visiting the forest or ocean. Perhaps you will begin daily meditation.

_____

_____

_____

_____

_____

_____

_____

_____

_____

_____

CHAPTER 21

THE VIRGIN

"I carefully analyse with love, acceptance and simplicity."

Sign: Virgo
Ruler: Mercury
Element: Earth
Season: Summer
Colour: Blue
Stone: Sapphire
Light elements: Attentive, Intelligent, Healing, Loving, Compassionate
Shadow elements: Over-thinking, Critical, Severe, Withdrawn, Irresponsible

When we journey through the 6th house of Virgo, we are facing our most potent medicine of all –self-love and healing. In this space, after we have danced, played, and created from the heart space, we are then called by Virgo's energy to be of service to ourselves. This transition is our place where we can truly meet our needs, asking ourselves what we require to be our most authentic selves, so that we can also be of service to others.

If we cannot love and nourish ourselves then we certainly cannot love and nourish others. If we are living in the shadows of all the other houses that come before Virgo then this is the place where the soul will transcend them. This is a place of love, freedom, healing, emotional intelligence, compassion and attentiveness. This is the place where we must honour our mind, body, and soul for us to become the best version of ourselves.

Those who are disconnected from self-love and being of service to themselves are most likely stuck in a state of critical over-thinking and analysing. These shadows are the very thing that will be the catalyst for great healing – especially when it comes to rebirthing the soul.

Rebirth asks the mind to slow down so that one can go within and feel into the heart and body. When this process is initiated, rebirth happens with flow, surrender and trust. Overthinking and too much analysing is often a response mechanism to avoid going through the process of rebirthing the soul. So many souls can get stuck in the never-ending cycle of being called to answer their needs and requirements here in the 6th house.

I believe that you are seen by the earth. You are cleansed by the ocean. You are heard by the stars. The universe is here, always supporting you in manifesting your greatest dreams. We do not need to over-think, judge or analyse – everything is already working out for us in divine timing.

Soul Communication

- ❖ What elements of the virgin's light are reflected in your life?
- ❖ What elements of the virgin's shadow are mirrored in your life?
- ❖ Do you serve yourself with the love and compassion you deserve?
- ❖ How can you share your light by being of service to others?

Now, let us talk about the word 'perfect'. We are living in times that move so sheepishly around the word 'perfect'. I have been that person who gives out endless compliments to others but dims her light the moment they return.

I have seen it in my friends and so many other men and women. It is as if we are crippled by the idea of celebrating our greatness, because far too often this has been mistaken for narcissism. But we must shine our light and do so brightly.

As humans, we need some sort of physical evidence to accept the idea that we are seamless beings; that our existence is eternal in its very magnitude. But through the language of the soul, we can somehow be reminded in a strange and yet so familiar way that we are indeed perfect beings and we do not need any evidence to prove this.

For decades, the likes of modern media have captured us within some sort of body image bust-up. There are far too many men and women trapped in a matrix of not feeling good enough. This has resulted in judgemental perceptions of us and those around us.

It is as if we are at the edge of a cliff. A cliff that is crumbling. We cannot hold on much longer. And because of this crumbling, the truth is being revealed. We are fast discovering that we are enough, through the simple return to our soul's mission and align with universal source.

During the sharp and painful process of removing layers that once created a false sense of self, we can, and we will discover that we are so much more than just the way we look. We are much greater than that.

Beauty goes beyond the all-seeing eye. Beauty lives in our ability to create, our authenticity, pure in its moral compass. Beauty is both the creation of new and destruction of old, gifted to us in our life. Beauty is the rawest part of your very own magnificence which you must embody each day.

Allow yourself to be pulled into the matrix long enough and you will be dealing with a whole lot of smoky mirrors. The further one is pulled into the matrix of comparison, the harder it is to get out. We must cut through the rubbish and remember the truth in our hearts. Know that you are beautiful regardless of what is being communicated in society.

To truly break free from the societal chains that often portrays a sense of 'not good enough', we require a whole lot of trust and even a glimpse of courage to step forward and simply focus on our own energy. Where will you find the trust and courage to be whole in your genuine beauty? When you actively participate in the cleansing of the soul, setting the intention of what makes you feel internally beautiful. Every. Single. Day.

You do not need Photoshop to modify the size of your body. You do not need to turn to anything or anyone outside of yourself to validate who you are or what you do.

Your soul cares that you have wholesome food to eat, fresh air to breathe, clean water to drink and a roof over your head. Your soul wants the best for you. It wants deeply connected relationships. It wants adventure. It wants creativity, culture, books, and the ocean. Your soul recognises the true beauty of life through higher vibrational frequencies of unconditional love.

As one attempts to amend something that does not even need amending, they can become fixated on the search to amend another. It's sad to see so many people spend their entire lives attempting to reshape and redefine their 'not-enough-ness', only to get to the end of their life and realise they were perfection and beauty from the beginning.

I once had a friend tell me, *"It's okay Olivia, you can't be perfect all of the time,"* At the time I thought that was a great way to justify my failures. But you see, even failure is so perfect and does not need justification, and if that is possible then I can be perfect all the time.

If we are to truly be open to receive that which the soul is trying to communicate, then we must remember, every moment is unfolding in perfect order. The good, the bad, and the ugly. We must know in the depth of our hearts that every moment of life is a moment of perfection. By fuelling the mind, body and soul with positive affirmations, it is the law of the universe to respond.

Soul Communication

- ❖ What story are you telling yourself each day?
- ❖ What areas in your life might your story need re-writing?
- ❖ Do you need to create a new one that is more unconditionally aligned with love?

Even during the most difficult of moments, we can affirm that our perfection is forever present. The law of attraction is here to work with the promptings of your soul. In short, speak what you would prefer to feel and have in your life, then take a step back and leave the rest to the universe. You can move into a higher field of vibration and it is the law of the universe to respond.

Trust that your soul never lies. Trust that the world, now more than ever, needs you to affirm your perfect humanness. Trust that even in the most difficult moments of darkness, your higher self is always planning the best intentions, in a quest for your return to wellbeing. When you trust in this higher power you allow your mind, body and soul to work with the rhythms of higher vibration. When you work with the rhythms of a higher vibration you are saying yes to living from the purity of your soul. You are saying a huge yes to unlimited abundance.

Do the bees stop collecting nectar from the flowers because there are clouds in the sky? Do the birds stop flying because they have lost the courage to use their wings? We know that lions do not question their existence – they roar anyway. We know that fish do not contemplate their role in the ocean – they swim anyway. So why humans? It is noticeably clear to see the most detrimental action we will ever take is to deny our unique inner landscape. To forget that our answers come from within, is to forget the limitless source of light that we are.

And so here we are, painting over this beautiful picture that once beamed all its unique colour. Here we are, building layers over the inner glory that once shined through when pure and unscathed as a child. And as we paint over and as we cover-up, we close off and we shut down. All we know is our physicality, abandoning emotional, mental, and spiritual nourishment, leaving us at dis-ease with who we are, the relationships we have and the work we do. This is not our birth-right; our birth-right is infinite, multidimensional love.

If we want to get to the root of the cause of dis-ease, then perhaps we must take a moment to explore the emotions that have been suppressed within. I am not saying that I know how to cure everyone's mental health concerns but what I am saying is that such limited belief systems manifest as disconnection from the soul and this is disconnection from life.

Feeling stuck with burdening beliefs such as 'not being enough' creates layers upon layers of conditioning. But the good news is that your soul is here to remove such rigid ways of thinking, through its divine expression of unconditional love. Surrender to the lies that you have been playing over and over. Surrender, surrender, and surrender once more. In this space of vulnerability, you will tear away all the false layers, leaving you with only the remains of purity – the purest parts of your soul.

Take a moment to read the invocation below. If you are serious about painting your new story of unconditional self-love, then read it each morning for six days in a row. Feel the power within each word move through your mind, body and soul – know that you are what you choose to be.

Soul Communication

Across time and space, I choose now to stand strong in my infinite perfection. I am enough and I am perfect in all my humanness. I open myself up to aligning with the purity of my soul and allow this unstoppable higher power of my birth-right to guide me in living a life that is rich and abundant. I surrender to all that I am not and align with the passion, values, and truth in my heart, allowing (you can state whatever you like here) to manifest into my reality. May all those who are suffering from limiting beliefs around their existence be reassured of their limitless love, beauty, abundance, and perfection. So be it!

CHAPTER 22

THE HEALING DIMENSION

"To love every part of yourself is the quietest, simplest, most powerful revolution – embody that."

It is your will that changes the world. Crashing through the depths of your darkest night of the soul, you opt for willingness; you opt to change the world anyway. It is your courage that brings strength to the world. Even if you feel a little lost or overwhelmed, you can always choose courage; you can always choose to bring strength to the world anyway. It is your wisdom that adds insight to the world. Even if you are entangled in the uncertainty that may have left you feeling confused and broken, you can always search for your wisdom; you can pour your insight into the world anyway. It is your wounds and your scars that transform this world. Even though you have been hurt by the people and events that taught you pain, you can share your healed heart; you can choose to bring love to the world anyway.

Love. The most mysterious and powerful force in the universe. If there is one thing the soul knows – its love. Love connects everything. Love heals everything.

But for many decades there has been some misconception around the term self-love. While we have the mass media making billions of dollars through playing on people's low self-esteem around body image, we are also – far too often – feeling guilty about serving ourselves with non-negotiable self-love.

Self-love is the miracle cure. When you serve yourself, you can serve everyone and everything in your life. Self-love is the miracle cure because it lights up the greatest, most authentic parts of oneself. It is what the soul resonates with. Love is what brought you here and where you shall return to. If we are to search for answers and find solutions, we shall find it in love.

Self-love includes saying no to the distractions, quitting jobs that cause more stress than create joy, getting a one-way ticket across the globe to explore new territory, or ending a toxic relationship.

So, what is the key to living an abundant life through the act of completely loving who you are and embodying every part of your humanness? For me, it is trust. For you, it might be confidence. When we trust in ourselves and we own our uniqueness with confidence, we can begin to walk a path of self-worth.

I am sure you already know this, but I would like to remind you once more: you cannot give others what you cannot give yourself.

CHAPTER 23

SOUL ALIGNMENT

"You think it's the end, but this is just the beginning."

Imagine investing years of money, energy, passion, love, work and dedication into a dream. Imagine spending your heart and soul on a perfect dream, only to have the whole thing completely crumble in front of your eyes. Imagine having the entire foundations you have built over time swiped away from you.

In October 2017, I packed my suitcase and left behind my Australia dream. I had been creating and investing in this vision for many years. However, after a relationship breakdown that had my soul entirely out of alignment, I was left with two choices.

Number one – stay and continue building on top of unstable foundations that would eventually crumble and force me to let go later. Number two – surrender and let go of absolutely everything, right there, right now, trusting that love will, again, guide me to a new beginning of something far more magnificent.

I chose the latter.

I chose the second option, and it was not easy, but it certainly was worth it.

It was not easy because there is nothing easy about quitting a job that you enjoy. There is nothing easy about moving out of an apartment that feels like your sanctuary. There is nothing easy about leaving a country that you love and saying goodbye to friends that you are so intricately connected to. There is nothing easy about being pushed to cut ties with everything because it is forced upon you by a psychological struggle.

The spirit of the divine feminine was rising within me. My cousin was travelling around New Zealand at the time, so I chose to join her, bringing about a powerful sense of newness and liberation. I set off to this beautiful country at the end of the year, feeling called to the pure land, where the goddess went into retreat in the dark ages. They say that travel is as much about exploring your inner world as your outer world. It was time for me to go within. It was time for me to meet my inner divine feminine nature.

When I arrived, I felt like I had lost absolutely everything. However, I was now living on a blank, clean slate which felt quite freeing from the past struggles of the toxic relationship.

The problem arrived a few months later when I recognised that while I had let go of everything externally, I was going through an internal battle. There was something strong that called for me to go through a process of healing.

The only thing that remained was the dedication I had made to following the highest vibrational calling of love that lived in my soul. I so desperately wanted to free myself from the blame, anger, shame and resentment that was associated with my ex-partner. Forgiveness for the fact that our relationship had become lost in the abyss of darkness. It felt like a never-ending road and I lost a lot of sleep over the stress of what a quarter-life crisis can bring.

Now that I had chosen to pack up everything and leave, it was time for me to face my darkest moments to date.

The truth can sometimes be painful, but it will always set you free. When you have sponsorship to remain in a country that is not your home country, because your partner is primarily the reason why you have a visa, you feel called to be true to yourself every single day. You feel called to reminisce in the integrity of love, and how it is the most dynamic force in the universe that the soul needs to feel whole. But after years of feeling more disconnected than ever, I realised that I did not have this wholeness. The truth is that every relationship I have ever had, has simply been a reflection of myself. When we break-off and run away from others, we are running away from ourselves. I am grateful that he taught me this lesson, for he was simply mirroring all the parts of myself that I rejected, denied and suppressed.

When we love and accept others without judgement, we love and accept ourselves. When we forgive others for their mistakes, we forgive ourselves too. That is true freedom. That is the embodiment of love – seeing through the eyes of the soul.

Perhaps experiences like this happen because the universe has a plan to make us stronger so that we can create something bigger and better. Perhaps experiences like this happen because if we do not feel genuinely aligned with that person or relationship, then maybe it was only supposed to be for a chapter. Perhaps experiences like this happen because it is merely transpiring for the more significant development of the soul – a higher purpose.

Each day I am grateful for this person pushing me to leave Australia when our relationship broke down. Not just because it was immigration's rules for me to depart, but because I needed to go through the healing progression of rebirthing my soul. I needed to be true to myself and step into living from a more courageous heart space.

If he did not push me along my way, then I would not have expanded into the resilient person that I am today. If he did not push me along my way, then I would not have faced some of my darkest demons and fears that once controlled me. If he did not push me along my way, later, I would not have awakened to recognise how especially important the rebirthing process is. If he did not push me along my path, then I would not have met my twin soul, who I am truly blessed to have by my side, teaching me unconditional love every single day. Each day I am grateful for this karmic lesson.

So thank you, karma, for bringing this person into my life to show me the most profound lesson of how we must surrender to rebirth, for there is where we shall unlock the potent medicine that is forgiveness and love. And this is not just forgiveness and love for the self, but for everyone and everything on the entire planet. Thank you, universe, for showing me that there is love after loss, and that darkness can be transcended to light.

Such transcendence can happen if only we remember to tap into the language of the soul, recognising that life is a cyclic process of death and rebirth. Transcendence can happen, but we first must recognise that astrology is not so much about some psychic woman telling you that tomorrow you will buy a red car and meet the love of your life. Astrology is a tool for understanding the metaphorical process of rebirthing and evolving the many dimensions that exist within your life. We are not one zodiac sign – we are all of them. Each house represents a different element within our soul's journey and when we discover that each sign plays a significant role within our life, we can be reminded – every single day – that we are all one, united through a beautiful force of love and oneness. Unity is our birth-right and this astrological journey proves exactly that.

Where your sun, moon and rising sign is associated, reflects a more reliable connection to that specific sign. However, that does not mean that the other signs have nothing to do with you. The soul journeys through every sign and every house throughout life. This story shows you that we must honour all placements because they all dramatically reflect the cycle of life, and rebirthing of the soul. Instead of identifying yourself with one placement, this metaphor will enable you to recognise that you can identify with the entire spectrum. That is the purpose of Soul Communication – reminding us that when all is said and done, we are united. We are united because each sign plays a role in our life.

CHAPTER 24

THE 6ᵀᴴ SOUL COMMUNICATION

"Your soul is a force of limitless love, powerful in all of its creations."

Find a quiet space for yourself and breathe deep into your lungs.

Centre yourself in this present moment. Put one hand on your heart and close your eyes. Feel the ground below you, holding you in its gravitational pull.

Ask the wisdom of your heart, *"What messages do you have for me in this given moment?"*

Remain here until you have moved deep enough down into your soul space. Hold it and breathe into this place of trust and clarity for a few more moments. As you breathe, visualise your inner-world and how bright its light can shine. Be open to allowing your intuition to come through. In this space, you can affirm that you are ready to receive guidance from the heart. Sink into your stillness so that all truth and messages from your higher self can be brought to the surface.

Trust that whatever comes through, is for your highest good.

Remain here for as long as you like. When you have finished in this space, bring your centred and grounded clarity back to the room, present in your body, calm in your mind, and soft in your body.

Finish by completing the following script below.

The best form of love I can give to myself is:

_____

_____

_____

_____

_____

_____

_____

_____

_____

When I serve myself first, I can achieve the following:

_____

_____

_____

_____

_____

_____

_____

_____

_____

_____

I set boundaries by saying no to the following things:

_____

_____

_____

_____

_____

_____

_____

_____

_____

These boundaries serve me because:

_____

_____

_____

_____

_____

_____

_____

_____

_____

Olivia Blakey

I check in with my overall feelings of wellbeing each day by:

_____

_____

_____

_____

_____

_____

_____

_____

_____

I am committed to:

_____

_____

_____

_____

_____

_____

_____

_____

_____

Because this makes me feel:

_____

_____

_____

_____
_____
_____
_____
_____
_____
_____

One act of self-love I do each day is:

_____
_____
_____
_____
_____
_____
_____
_____
_____

Which enables me to:

_____
_____
_____
_____
_____
_____
_____

Olivia Blakey

_____

_____

_____

It is acceptable to completely honour my mind, body, and spirit because:

_____

_____

_____

_____

_____

_____

_____

_____

_____

_____

CHAPTER 25

THE SCALES

"I balance my mind and body with the callings of my soul."

Sign: Libra
Ruler: Venus
Element: Air
Season: Fall
Colour: Green
Stone: Marble
Light elements: Sociable, Accommodating, Understanding, Connected, Balanced
Shadow elements: Blocked, Stagnant, Unforgiving, Unfair, Self-centred

When the soul journeys through the 7th house, we are being called to the soulful evolution of our relationships. This is not just relationships with others, but with the self too. The 7th house is a place of love and belonging that is ruled by the planet Venus. The question is not so much about what we are connected to, but rather, who we are connected to.

The house of Libra is a place for transcending all that we see as darkness, into light. After fully serving ourselves and others in the house of Virgo, we are then brought to this place of relationships and interconnectedness.

When I was going through my process of rebirth, it took me three solid years to shake off a dark trip that I felt trapped within. While my earlier years were quite chaotic in terms of my social circles, I was later being called to develop a better relationship with myself, spending more time in solitude to nourish my soul and invest my energy into forging a more authentic life path.

The truth is, you can have a lot of people in your external circle, but the real gems are those within your inner circle.

Just before I entered my quarter-life crises, I came to recognise that I was spending far too much energy on relationships that did not serve me. It wasn't just chaotic, it was absolutely exhausting and only when I was forced to slow down and recognise this truth, did I realise that I had not been truly in charge of my own energy – it was wasted in time and places, with people that were not in alignment with the callings of my soul.

Some people come into our lives for a chapter, some a season and some a lifetime. Those who are not on our path for long usually play a role in teaching a lesson and being catalysts for propelling us into a new direction. These types of relationships are just as valuable as the long-term ones, so long as we learn to live from non-attachment, holding on for too long out of fear of letting go.

When I arrived back in Australia in November 2019, I had undergone a spiritual cleansing and craved union with my soul family who I knew were out there waiting for me.

I had no idea where I would find my soul family, but I trusted that the universe would deliver in divine timing.

One Sunday evening, I ventured out with a close friend of mine who had always been a huge part of my life. We have always been aligned in the soul because we both value the importance of health on all levels. My younger years with Kat were surrounded by partying until the early hours of the morning but we were not so much doing this anymore – we were learning to live in balance and moderation.

That night, we re-lived some of our best moments at a Sydney nightclub that we had always loved, sticking around until the early hours of the morning, doing what we had not done in a while. When Kat and I dance, we are completely in sync with the universe and music feeds our soul with pure medicine.

"Where's the after-party?" one of our friends asked, who was supposed to be heading off to work in a couple of hours. As we laughed about the fact, he was on the dance floor with his alarm for work going off, we decided we were having a big one. The sun was rising but we weren't going to stop the tequila flowing, and thank goodness we chose to free our soul that night with a carefree attitude, because it led me further along my path to the gold I was waiting for; my soul family.

Not only did I meet my twin soul at the after-party, I met his Italian soul family. These people are now the reason I flow with the words of this book because not only have they reminded me the power of music and how it brings people together, they have also reminded me just how important it is to follow the medicine that aligns your soul.

I honestly do not know a single person who does not like music. The art and medicine of music is potently healing for the mind, body and soul, but also a universal language which brings people together. Music plays such a powerful role in the house of Libra, for it is the light that weaves the web of relationships and brings humanity together in perfect vibrational harmony.

If we are living in the shadows of the 7th house, then it is often because we are feeling disconnected from our soul family and we have not yet aligned with their vibration. By the time we have reached the scales component, we are being called to recognise where our light is shining on the concept of relationships.

Those who are blocked, stagnant, unforgiving, unfair, and self-centred are often disconnected from their most authentic vibration. When living in the shadows of Libra, we are often called to being more creative and socially connected within our lives so that we can transmute the fear and darkness to love and light.

This is also a powerful place that reflects the role of the previous house – Virgo. If your relationship with yourself and service to yourself is that which is unaligned with love, then how are you supposed to attract your soul family? Those who are stuck in the shadows will attract nothing more than those who are also stuck in the shadows, which serves an immensely powerful lesson for the great need to transcend.

Soul Communication

❖ Are you shining your light so that your soul family can find you?
❖ Are you stuck in the shadows, attracting karmic lessons from those who are not your soul family?
❖ What does the vibrational match of your soul family look and feel like?
❖ How can you align with them?

CHAPTER 26

THE RELATIONSHIP DIMENSION

*"I call my soul family into my inner circle –
I call my soul tribe into my world."*

I made my way back to Australia on a student visa to study an Advanced Diploma in Leadership and Management. I had plans in place to start over, but no way did I realise that my light was shining so powerfully. I was shocked at how potent the soul work had been. I had spent three years reshaping myself, releasing identities that no longer served me, left with only the purest truths of myself and my callings. I had spent a lot of time with myself, doing the inner work within the house of Virgo. After the crumbling tower moment of my shadows erupting, being forced to start over, it took me a long time to journey through the houses of understanding where in my life I needed to transcend my fears into restored love.

Much of my life had been shaped by attracting karmic lessons from people that were not my soul family. I was twenty-six years old and this crumbling of old paradigms felt like the end of my world, yet I had to face the truth that most of my relationships in my life were not serving my soul. Many of the relationships that I attracted were, in fact, reflecting the toxicity of my inner world and the inability to serve myself with the self-love and self-care that every soul needs.

It is no surprise that one who cannot serve themselves through the lessons of Virgo, can remain stuck there for their entire life, refusing the call to rebirth. For the soul to continue in the abundant flow of its cyclic evolutionary process, there is a potent lesson about shining the light on oneself before one can move forward and shine their light on their external relationships. When my life crumbled in front of my eyes, I recognised that the most vital element of life is the relationship with self. You cannot expect to attract the highest vibration of your soul family if you are not honouring what is required to have a healthy relationship with yourself.

Soul Communication

❖ What is your relationship with yourself?
❖ How does your relationship with yourself reflect in your relationship with others?

I came back to Australia in 2019 because I had unfinished business with this country. Three years later I was back in the same place repeating the same story which had become my reality, but this time, I had risen like a phoenix from the ashes, and I was seeing through the eyes of my unconditional loving, divine soul. I had carried through much wisdom from my rebirthing journey and my alignment felt strong.

Your soul family must find you – one way or another. They are out there, and they are calling for you to find them in every single moment. You align with the vibration of your soul family when you become aligned with the callings of your heart and that which truly matters in your life.

Soul families are healing and bring about massive shifts in your creative essence, driving you towards your soul's mission that has been destined to manifest during your entire existence on the planet.

It is not so much a question of where your soul family are, for they are everywhere and always ready to meet you. The question is when you will become aligned with what truly matters in your life so that you can find these people and become a part of their tribe.

It does not matter what type of creator you are; what matters is that you are in total alignment with your creations. Whether you work with food, people, animals, technology, or astrology, the truth lies within the hearts of what your vibration is.

I found my soul family through simply being in configuration with the things that brought out the best in my career and lifestyle – that was writing, creativity, music, and horses.

We do not have to feel alone. For as long as we are on this planet, all we must do is look around. One million and more pointers are directing us towards the people and places that serve our higher self.

Soul Communication

- ❖ Where are you shining your light so that your soul family can find you?
- ❖ How can you transcend your darkness to call in your soul family?
- ❖ What areas in your life are reflecting soulful relationships and what areas are reflecting karmic return?

CHAPTER 27

THE BALANCED SOUL

"The secret is not so much about searching for what or who you are. Rather, it is about recognising and uncovering what you are not, so that you can arrive at your most authentic truth, your birth-right of love. Through the process of stripping away layers, you will be guided back home, to your roots, in balance with your infinite source; guided to your soul."

Often, when one finally meets the calling of their soul, they tend to become aware of the wounds that once held them back. Through uncovering these wounds and freeing oneself from the limitations they hold, this calls for great forgiveness and releasing all judgement. It becomes clear within a metaphorical aspect that often the gun that is being pointed at others, is the gun that has been pointing at the self.

Your soul is a mirror, echoing all parts of yourself and everyone in your life. Every single one of your relationships, positive or negative is the most powerful way to see what is present and absent within your soul.

The things you love most in others are the things you love most in yourself. The things you dislike most in others are the things you deny most in yourself. We can be guided to our hearts' deepest callings through holding space to understand our biggest triggers and greatest attraction in the simple yet so powerful process of connecting with other souls. It is a gift to share this planet with other souls.

These people are here to reflect all parts of your soul and vice versa. Our most challenging and enlightening relationships are the most significant gift we will ever encounter since these connections are here to heal wounds as well as strengthen our inner magic.

So many of us are caught up in the role of victim and perpetrator, but perhaps time is the greatest truth seeker within this misconception. Often, we can appreciate the opportunity that was being presented to us to help our soul grow and evolve when the situation becomes a distant memory. It is through following forgiveness that we can begin to see the bigger picture and understand that nobody is the victim, and nobody is the perpetrator; we are all just teachers and students.

In honouring the knowledge and wisdom that can be attained through the power of reflection, we can relentlessly participate in the evolutionary journey of the soul – we can break free from our inner conflict, without judging others because we accept ourselves entirely.

Since these challenges are here to both trigger and enlighten you, drawing out the remainder of your wounds; these people are necessarily a gift – they are here to help you evolve, by merely being themselves.

Soul Communication

- ❖ What are your triggers?
- ❖ Why are you feeling triggered?
- ❖ How can you allow the triggers to be your most profound messages?
- ❖ How can you apply healing to transcend these triggers into something more positive?

When we choose to identify with our vulnerability, we open ourselves up to an invitation from the universe—a call to receive healing, a positive energy flow, and a whole lot more alignment. But being vulnerable is far from easy.

Soul Communication

- ❖ How can we integrate our vulnerability into relationships?
- ❖ How can we master this act of both standing strong in power as well as surrendering to the reflective lessons in relationships?

While being exposed to the rawest parts of oneself scares the hell out of many people, it is the very thing that will activate the return to unified authenticity. Once you have grasped the concept that everyone is merely an enabler, the daily practice of connecting with your soul will show you that you can indeed be your teacher, your challenger, and truth seeker. You are complete in your wholeness.

The moment one can remain anchored in their truth – their humanness – is the moment one's relationship with others moves from a place of karma to dharma. Connections become a motion of flourishing and thriving union.

CHAPTER 28

THE 7TH SOUL COMMUNICATION

"I honour the gift of sharing this planet with other souls."

Who are the people in your life that support and uplift your ideas, goals and dreams?

_____

_____

_____

_____

_____

_____

_____

_____

_____

_____

Why are you a vibrational match to these people – why do you connect well with them?

_____

_____

_____

_____

_____

_____

_____

_____

_____

"My soul can tap into unlimited potential."

Complete the following tasks to anchor positive energy into the integration of your masculine and feminine polarities. Remember there is no right or wrong answer. This is the journey of *your* soul.

What does 'doing' mean to you? Give examples of where you forcefully 'do' too much in your life.

_____

_____

_____

_____

_____

_____

_____

_____

_____

_____

What does 'being' mean to you? Give examples of where you can simply 'be' more in your life.

_____

_____

_____

_____

_____

_____

_____

_____

What would you like to create/manifest?

_____

_____

_____

_____

_____

_____

_____

_____

How does creating/manifesting this mission make you feel and why?

_____

_____

_____

_____

_____

_____

_____

Explain how you become a powerful creator in alignment with your soul when your mindset is in partnership with your emotions.

_____

_____

_____

_____

_____

_____

_____

_____

_____

Soul Communication

Across time and space, I choose now to be in a harmonious balance between my feminine and masculine energy. I honour both my darkness and light, allowing all emotions to come through. My emotions are my gift. May all those who are trapped in a state of disharmony be reconnected to their inner truth and guided by the wholeness of their soul. So be it!

List ten quality traits of your masculine energy. For example, focused, direct or passionate. See chapter thirty-eight – 'The Masculine Dimension' if needed.

_____

_____

_____

_____

_____

_____

_____

_____

_____

_____

List ten qualities of your feminine energy. For example, creative, flowing or nurturing. See chapter fourteen – 'The Feminine Dimension' if needed.

_____

_____

_____

_____

_____

Olivia Blakey

_____

_____

_____

_____

I feel a balance between feminine and masculine when I am fulfilling:

_____

_____

_____

_____

_____

_____

_____

_____

_____

_____

CHAPTER 29

THE SCORPION

"I desire to be in complete alignment with my soul."

Sign: Scorpio
Ruler: Pluto
Season: Autumn
Zodiac Sign: The 8th House
Colour: Purple
Stone: Opal
Light elements: Passionate, Psychic, Resourceful, Determined, Creative
Shadow elements: Fixed, Possessive, Deceitful, Fearful, Consuming

When we journey through to the 8th house of Scorpio, we are journeying through the most powerful dimension of rebirthing the soul. This is not just a place of giving all-new life, but metaphysically dying to old ways that no longer serve us.

The light that is present within the 8th house is passionate, physical, resourceful, determined, and creative. This is a place where we can wholly learn to let go of the old programs and open to the rejuvenation of life, living in alignment with the purity of the soul.

When we are living in the shadows of Scorpio, we are resisting the process of soulful healing and the opportunity to go through the process of rebirth. We are fixed, possessive, deceitful, fearful of endings, and life tends to feel like it is consuming us. These shadow elements must be transmuted if we are to move forward into the next dimension of Sagittarius where love is present after a loss. The next phase – Sagittarius – is where we learn that love and life is possible after being trapped in the illusion of fear. We can be reborn after a metaphysical death, just like the butterfly emerges from its cocoon where the struggle has previously happened.

The scorpion is potent medicine, delivering a dark night of the soul that holds the purpose of enabling us to go into the deepest introspection.

It is an element of life that many of us would rather not face, but if we are open to receiving the medicine of change with love, then the newness that is born gives rise to an exciting adventure.

The 8th house brings forth the illusion of a black tunnel. Often, we see things outside of ourselves as detrimental when really, all that we are supposed to do is release the limiting programming that is happening within the mind. When we release our limiting beliefs, we begin to recognise that everything outside of us is what we have asked to manifest within life.

No longer can we be victims of our circumstances for these are the very things that have shaped us. These are the things that we have asked to emerge within our lives so that we can learn and grow.

The scorpion's energy has always run wildly within my family. I have one brother and two cousins all born on the same day. Their energy is deeply intuitive and creative.

Scorpions know the truth because they are anchored in the dark night where transcendence is in its purest form. They are natural healers with deeply intuitive and empathic abilities. Their inner world is born from the concept of shamanism which is recognised throughout history as 'the one who knows'.

Since scorpion energy brings about intense opportunity for transformation, this is where the shamanic energy operates. Mystical and magical energy, it is a place where we come to face our deepest and darkest fears, breaking through the chains of what has always held you back.

Again, I would like to emphasise that this is the most potent medicine of all, for our shadows are where we can dig deep to find our most authentic creativity, transforming the darkness to light. Scorpio strength is born from the watery depths of the ocean. The Scorpion is the second to last water element that holds the wisdom before finally reaching its sister sign, to go through the ending of all to reach the most spiritual dimension – Pisces.

If anything, we must learn to love the black tunnels that we have created in our mind rather than shutting them out. We must ask ourselves why we have created such rigidity in the first place and how we can embrace life with a renewed sense of limitless power.

The shadow elements of the scorpion often represent taboo topics such as death. The connection to death seems rather daunting but when you surrender to this dark night, you soon discover that there is life after death and love after loss. You can sail your ship through this rebirth dimension knowing that great things are waiting ahead of you. You can swim in the ocean, free like a mermaid, without fearing the monsters and demons that have created such a fearful illusion. You can learn to fully embody unconditional love for everyone and everything in your life.

CHAPTER 30

THE REBIRTH DIMENSION

"You can lose absolutely everything, but you will never lose the divinity of your soul."

Fear is false evidence appearing real. Some say that fear holds the purpose of awakening you from the illusion of being separate so that you can embody oneness. Others say that fear holds the purpose of bringing one back to a state of pure love. Perhaps fear is a way of reminding us that we must journey inwards to remember that light is the only truth. Or perhaps fear is the catalyst for our evolution.

Rejecting, denying, and suppressing the things we fear most, is the fastest way to create more fear in one's life. Instead, we must nurture our fears and overcome them by doing the very thing that scares the hell out of us, because that is when rebirth effortlessly unfolds for the better. That is when one recreates a life of love, joy and abundance.

The black tunnel is an illusion – an illusion created by the limiting beliefs that are programmed within the mind, gathered from all past experiences of pain and suffering. When one is journeying through what is known as the black tunnel, they must uncover the only truth to make their way out; the truth is that the soul only knows and embraces love.

The black tunnel is also an illusion because for as long as one remains in this state of consciousness, the mind remains disconnected from the soul's mission, remembering its divinity and limitless ability to weave love into the web of life.

It is no surprise that the current state of mental health concerns is on the rise, increasing within western society. A topic with harsh labels that is driven by concepts of the patriarchy is on its way to a new path that is more aligned with unity, healing, and oneness. This is the rise in divine feminine energy awakening within us which I have already spoken about. This new path is being forged because the values of the patriarchy which include hierarchy, competition and attempting to push and strive alone, is no longer working. We are being forced to rebirth in a new way. This new way is the language of the soul.

Transformational journeys of coming into alignment with the soul can often bring about immense struggle and the feeling of needing to resist, rather than surrender. This is because humans, often programmed by past experiences, would rather hold onto what they know instead of embracing the unknown. In short, unfamiliar territory can bring about immense fear and often leaves one stuck in a repetitive cycle that is attempting to be transformed.

Fear might be an illusion, but fear is our greatest teacher, catalyst and enabler. Fear can bring about immense healing if we are to dive deep into our inner child element of self and reclaim his/her playfulness as well as heal and release negative experiences that have been stored in our psychological memory. For a beautiful journey in the transcendence of fear to love, it is required for one to recognise that they no longer must suffer unless they choose to.

The purpose of our existence is to evolve the collective soul of humanity. I believe that this evolution is guiding us to living our most authentic life – but first – we must transcend all fear to love. When all is said and done, it is fair to say that there is one truth that remains: we are all waves from the same ocean.

We are one consciousness experiencing itself subjectively, and it is our mission to remember this. When we remember this, we reclaim our power, enabling us to live a life that is free from suffering, not because challenges will never arrive again, but because our greatest challenges often require the rebirthing process which is the very tool for releasing the old and receiving the new.

Be it pain or joy, not only does everything happen for a reason, everything happens for our unique unfolding of evolution. The more we go through, the more we grow and hold the capacity to come into alignment with the soul when dealing with difficult and challenging times.

If we are all divine light beings housed in human bodies and we were born from love, then love is our birth-right throughout our entire existence.

It must be recognised that all fear-based thinking is an illusion made up by the ego, often created to protect itself. When this limiting story is recognised in the rise of awareness and the process of psychological death, the soul can go on to live a life of love, abundance, and harmony. You can live a life of alignment that is on your own terms, rather than being driven by the pain of past experiences.

I believe that everyone's soul knows exactly what lessons each of us intend to learn whilst navigating the earth realm – it is some sort of mission planned before journeying through the cosmic womb. The moment we enter our human home is the moment that we are born to remember the power of love – we must face our fears if we are destined to remember this truth. Most importantly, we must accept what we fear most to be free from the prisons of our minds that are often constructed of blocks, negative belief systems, and limiting patterns. It must also be noted that the soul emanates from pure love and only wants the best for you here in this lifetime – rebirth may appear to be challenging, but it is the evolutionary process of your soul and it sure is worth it.

Living a life that is conditioned by fear is a coping mechanism for the ego. It is a lower vibrational frequency that is often manifested from past experiences, but it must be recognised that when we block ourselves off from one thing, we block ourselves off from everything. We must accept the past, forgive ourselves and others, as well as focus on recreating a new story and programming of the mind, so that we can expand out into the universe.

Soul Communication

- ❖ Where in your life are you repeating stories of the past?
- ❖ What new story would you like to create?
- ❖ Do you believe that you are the master of your mindset or do you just let life happen to you?

Fear serves a great purpose in the evolution of the soul.

After a while, we face our fears because we can no longer avoid them. We would rather feel liberated by our fears than feel trapped by them. We would rather evolve from our fear than remain stuck in its frequency, never truly moving forward to attain what we need. We won't always get what we want, but we sure will get what we need – and that always turns out to be the best thing ever. We would rather embrace our fears than never discover where they lead us to. We would rather our fears excite us then live a life that is mundane and boring. We would rather take leaps into living authentically, knowing that love is all there is, rather than giving our power away to false evidence appearing real.

Fear is the reason why so many people hold onto jobs they do not enjoy, and eventually quit to become their own cheerleaders doing what they love. Fear is the reason why people stay in relationships that they would rather not be in, only to discover they can meet someone far more loving and authentic when they finally ditch the one who is not in alignment. Fear is the reason so many choose to resist the flow of life, only to realise that when we resist the flow of life, we close off from our treasures and gold. Eventually, fear teaches us to let go because holding on is stopping one from living their most authentic life.

Soul Communication

❖ What are your fears teaching you?
❖ How are they guiding you towards living in alignment with your soul's mission?
❖ What would transform in your life if you were to truly embrace your deepest fears?
❖ What must you release and let go of to transcend fear to love?

Would you like to know the purpose of love? While love certainly unites all, it can be a subjective experience for everybody. One thing is for sure though; love sets you free. Love helps you to evolve. Love opens your eyes. Love is in everything and everywhere.

Soul Communication

❖ Do you believe that love is your greatest energetic tool?
❖ Are your thoughts programmed with love?

❖ What area in your life is mostly shaped by love?

❖ How can you recreate more love in other areas of your life?

So many of us want to avoid the pain that is presented to us because losing the things that we hold on to (that no longer serve us), can often feel like we are going to die. But for as long as we fear death, we push away the beauty, love, and joy that is calling us. It is our divine birthright to experience unconditional love, in this earth realm. It can be an unfortunate journey for the majority who are attached to the belief systems that the ego has made up.

I have once been a victim of fear, enduring such grief, but I have learned there is a way to overcome how we deal with this and it certainly does not have to continue throughout an entire lifetime.

In 1992 I was born in a small town called Grimsby in the northeast of the United Kingdom. Like many of us, when we become aware of our sense of self, we are like sponges, soaking up every piece of knowledge and information that comes to us. Before we are born on earth, I completely believe that we have a mission to fulfil – our mission can only be fulfilled if we learn the lessons that are presented to us. If we open ourselves up to what is being taught, then we can begin to find our true calling – we can find the things in life that truly matter; we can live our dharma.

In my younger years, I was not held in the arms of my mother for long. She was unable to give me the love and comfort that all children need. My mother has carried many deep wounds from her past throughout her life and the way this has wounded her, was projected onto myself and others.

Not only did I feel abandoned when she walked out on my father, leaving him in turmoil, I could feel her suffering from abandonment too. Her mother – my grandmother – battled with mental illness –the rebirthing process – and chose to take her own life when my mother was just a teenager. My grandfather was also suffering from his wounds, projecting his anger onto my grandmother with violent behaviour.

Let it be clear that every action creates an entire ripple, influencing the web of the universe.

I so desperately wanted to have my mother in my life, but she was unavailable for me. I carried this pain with me, and it reflected in all areas of my life. My relationships were abusive because the relationship with myself was abusive. I pushed so hard, overworking, because I pushed so hard on myself. I often destroyed things that came onto my path out of fear of inviting intimacy into my life.

By the time I turned twenty-six, this stopped. This stopped because the universe forced me to open my eyes and look at the destruction that I was painfully manifesting in my life. The universe taught me the power of rebirth as I chose to press the reset button. My soul was ready to forge a new path; one of unconditional love, not just for myself but for everyone and everything in my life.

The bottom line is that we can choose to play the role of victim living a story of abandonment over and over, letting its fear ooze out in all areas of life. Or we can see through the eyes of love, breaking the cycle to write a completely new story; one that is aligned with devotion. We can use our past traumas to let go of fear and grow into wise souls embodying authenticity.

The soul has journeyed through lifetimes upon lifetimes. You might think that this is the first time you have resided on earth, but you have probably been here many, many times. It is the journey of the soul that enables the evolution of the universe – you are not separate from this universe, but in fact, *you are the universe.* The soul operates in 5-dimensional oneness – it is the navigator between spirit and matter.

When housed in the human body, the soul enters each lifetime through the portal of the cosmic womb; journeying to the earth realm to complete a mission and learn its most needed lessons to evolve. When the mind is in alignment with the callings of the soul, grounding the magic into matter unfolds, and we become vessels who are the creators of this magic. Whether we choose to manifest fear or love, it is our choice and that is the beauty of free will.

If you have journeyed through the rebirth process or are currently journeying through the black tunnel, know that your greatest power is the light of your soul, and throughout this book of intentionally aligning with love, you shall be guided to living a higher vibration of abundance and creativity. You are choosing to become the divine creator of your own life.

CHAPTER 31

THE DARK NIGHT

"Knowing your truth is one thing, but to live it is another."

The things we fear most are the things we need to do most. We often know what it is that we fear most but go through extreme ways of avoiding and denying those parts of ourselves because we would rather not confront the shadows. Humans are great at masking things that they would rather not face, but there can only be so long that these elements can be rejected and denied, locked up in the shadow parts of oneself. It is not long before the shadows emerge in unhealthy ways and we begin to recognise the things that we must transcend.

Just like the butterfly arises from its cocoon of struggle, once living as a caterpillar, spiritual and soulful transformation entails the exact same concept. The first step of stripping back the layers is often the place we would prefer to avoid. Many struggle to make it past this point because they would rather settle for what they know than step into unknown territory. But where is the fun in that? Life is supposed to be an adventure filled with joy, love and excitement. New beginnings are what bring zest into one's life.

Yet when you can find the courage to truly traverse such a fundamental journey, diving into the depths of your underworld, you will return with your elixir to share with the world. This transformative experience gives rise to ending a dark night of the soul which can be extremely crippling if we do not surrender to the process.

Living a life that sees beyond the veil seems confronting at first, but soon enough this becomes the beginning of seeing through all things and seeing into oneness – it is the journey that sets you free. It sets you free because you can cut through the dramas of the world; your elixir holds the key to redefining what life can truly be for you – not what others once told you. But first, you must set sail and draw on your inner warrior in all its resilience for the stormy weathers of the unknown. You must learn to swim in the deep waters of your soul, whether it be dark or light. You must trust in the process and remember that the universe will always have your back.

Know that this transition of shedding the old snakeskin is only temporary. If you are ever feeling stuck in the uncanny moment of crippling fear and unknown territory, then affirm: *"My transformation will bring me more love and it will be worth it."* Affirm this long enough and the words can become your truth. Soon enough you will discover that surrendering to the unknown is far easier than holding onto what you know. Eventually, we learn that there is great excitement that lives in the mystery of the unknown. So be open to it.

A dark night of the soul can last days, weeks, months and sometimes even years. For me, the process went on for longer than it should because I held on to my pain rather than choosing to let go. I needed to leave victimhood and leave fast. When I finally did, it was the most liberating feeling in the world, and I became great friends with the power of surrender.

The transition through spiritual awakening depends on how much we are willing to surrender. Surrender is trusting that even if we feel such a deep sense of loneliness, we are never truly alone.

When you reach this intense point of deep soul work and put time aside for introspection, be sure to use the **Dark Night Toolkit**. This will assist you in creating a less resistant journey to self-discovery, remaining as comfortable as possible through your transition. I created this for you, because it is something I have always turned to during extreme times of transformation. In short: compassion for the self during transformative times is deeply nurturing and healing, and deeply required.

Even as adults we are carrying our conditioning and programs from such a young age. All too often we are reacting out of scars that our inner child has not yet healed, and these shadows are what creates a dark night of the soul. If we are not in touch with our inner child, we can be trapped in a cycle of victimhood and self-sabotage that we will never truly be free from.

Through entering the sacred space of the heart and soul, we are essentially penetrating the infinity of oneself, where room for healing and awakening is always possible. To heal our inner child as well as surrender to our shadow selves, we must be willing to seek solutions that are new and empowered. We must solve our setbacks with a new mindset, as well as nurturing the most vulnerable parts of ourselves. Compassion everyone and everything is the key.

Perhaps when we feel such dis-ease about befriending our inner demons, we can turn to nature for answers. You see, if the flowers and trees, the birds and the bees resisted the change in seasons, then they simply would not exist. They could not possibly thrive and fulfil their purpose. Just like trees and flowers must lose their petals and the leaves in autumn to prepare for winter, we too must shed the skin of the old and prepare ourselves for metaphorical death as well as opening to a new life of rebirthing the soul. When we allow our old habits and ridged ways to psychologically die, we activate a sense of renewal and rejuvenation.

It certainly can be comforting to witness the simplicity of cyclic nature. I know that when I take a moment to observe the way nature works, it reminds me of the importance of fully being able to effortlessly surrender. Since we too are a product of nature, we must surrender to the rebirthing of the soul, ideas, belief systems and newness of life that is patiently waiting for us on the other side of fear.

To learn to die whilst you are alive is to traverse the realm of the psyche and shine light on all parts of oneself. To learn to die whilst you are alive is the journey to transcending all fear to love.

CHAPTER 32

THE 8ᵀᴴ SOUL COMMUNICATION

"In the darkest of nights, we find the illumination that is guiding us to our most authentic calling."

Dark Night Toolkit

❖ Drink plenty of water or herbal tea to flush out toxins released through the body's field of emotions.

❖ Eat vegetables, fruits, nuts, seeds, and protein to support your body, keeping it nourished as you work through the intensity of what emotions/beliefs come up to the surface.

❖ Take time to rest – rest more than usual. It is okay to take extra naps if necessary as it is important to honour the inner feminine during this time.

❖ Spend time in nature, by the ocean and/or connecting with animals.

❖ Put time aside for some gentle yoga and/or stretching – avoid strenuous activity – remember this is a time for slowing down.

❖ Avoid alcohol, caffeine, and/or any other harsh chemicals at all costs.

❖ Enjoy a massage or any other form of body therapy.

❖ Seek a therapist or mentor.

❖ If you need to cry, let the tears flow.

❖ When you feel stuck in a certain emotion, grab your pen and journal to express the way you feel. Try to focus on the things you are grateful for.

❖ Use an essential oil that supports your emotional wellbeing. Rose is great for moving through the shadow aspect of the self.

❖ Take a candle-lit, salted bubble bath to clear your energy field.

❖ Spend time in meditation, allowing your soul to bring forward its messages and guidance.

❖ Take part in a ritual that will strengthen your connection to a higher vibration – for me, sitting outside during the full moon and stargazing into the night is the queen of rituals.

❖ Listen to your favourite music that uplifts your senses.

❖ Sing, dance, and play to tap into the creativity of your pure and innocent inner child – simply be without expecting an outcome.

❖ Create and use affirmations to put positive signals out into the universe – what you send out will return.

❖ Take note of your dreams, trying to recall the messages from your subconscious.

❖ Spend time immersing in the therapy of art, whether this involves painting, drawing, cooking, or any other form of creating.

*"I choose to become a vibrational match to
the things I most desire in my life."*

I am willing to align with:

_____

_____

_____

_____

_____

_____

_____

_____

_____

_____

to create:

_____

_____

_____

_____

_____

_____

_____

_____

_____

_____

so that I can become:

_____

_____

_____

Olivia Blakey

_____

_____

_____

_____

_____

_____

_____

I feel in total alignment when I am:

_____

_____

_____

_____

_____

_____

_____

_____

_____

When I recognise that I am in total alignment, it makes me feel:

_____

_____

_____

_____

_____

_____

_____

_____

_____

_____

To remain in total alignment, I will focus on:

_____

_____

_____

_____

_____

_____

_____

_____

When I am in alignment, my outer world positively reflects:

_____

_____

_____

_____

_____

_____

_____

_____

_____

Olivia Blakey

Soul Communication

I surrender. I surrender to the perfection of all parts of myself and in allowing this perfection, I am fully held by Mother Earth. May all those who are consciously choosing to connect with their soul live in trust knowing they are supported. May the power of surrender lead us to infinite love, joy, and abundance. So be it!

CHAPTER 33

THE ARCHER

"I see unconditional love in everyone and everything. I believe in love after loss."

Sign: Sagittarius
Ruler: Jupiter
Element: Fire
Season: Autumn
Zodiac Sign: The 9th House
Colour: Turquoise
Stone: Topaz
Light elements: Optimistic, Enthusiastic, Adventurous, Honest, Independent
Shadow elements: Restless, Irresponsible, Dishonest, Co-dependent, Foolish

There is great power in the 9th house of the Archer. Sagittarius is known for its optimism, enthusiasm, adventure, honesty, and independence. Here is the place where we become most enlightened by discovering that our souls are limitless and can be reborn time after time. Here is the place where we bring forward all the wisdom we have learned through our losses. Here is the place where we can truly embody the richness of life itself.

The fire element of the Archer comes after the deep waters of the Scorpion where we have psychologically died to old ways and been through metamorphosis. This fire is the purest element of all, for it is said that ashes to ashes and dust to dust brings about the clearest form of divine energy.

When we travel through this fiery placement, we discover that not only are we boundless, but we can overcome anything if we have the fire in our heart. This is the residence where our soul is brought 'back to life' with all things possible showing up in the deepest corners of our hearts. It is almost like a journey back home to the self, where we are called to remember who we really were in the first elements of fiery Aries where our soul's identity was born. Not only can we teach others about the metaphor of life after death, but we can teach others that love is possible in all dimensions and realities. Love does not have to always be physical, for it can show up in the realm of spiritual transformation and learning to love the power of a healthy mindset.

When we are stuck in the shadows of Sagittarius, we are restless, irresponsible, dishonest, co-dependent, and foolish. These shadow elements can bring back patterns and behaviours of old ways, leaving the soul feeling stuck and unable to move forward. If we are to truly transcend these shadow elements into light then we will step up to be the teachers and leaders that we are supposed to be, expressing the truth of karma in all its ways. Karma is not what happens to us but rather, how we respond to all situations in life.

Sagittarius is symbolic of teaching, travel, philosophy, lessons, and afterlife. We often feel like we are stuck in a dirty mess when we resist the callings of Scorpio energy, but if we surrender to letting go of the old and create an invitation for the new, we can effortlessly traverse into the 9th dimension of Sagittarius where love and light is patiently waiting for us.

Here is a place of choice of responsibility. Will we step up and become the new leading version of ourselves, or will we lower the tone and keep it cool? The truth is that your soul desires for you to be a leader of the things that matter. Your soul wants you to level up and express love in all forms.

Working with horses taught me immense responsibility and I believe that their healing lessons are another reason why I wrote this book. It is not my responsibility to write this book because I plan to fuel my ego about being a powerhouse for overcoming such darkness. It is, rather, my responsibility to write this book to help others by sharing the wisdom that I have learned during my journey through rebirth. That is where I level up to being responsible and shining my Sagittarius light.

The same applies to you with your responsibility. The 9th house asks where you must step up in your life and to share your wisdom with the world. After all, we are here to help one another because that is exactly what will make the world a better place for us all. We can help one another and in the process of doing so, many rewards come flying in from the universe. Do the inner work and share your wisdom with those who need to hear your story because you never know what might come from it.

Soul Communication

- ❖ Do you focus on the love and renewal that is born after your losses?
- ❖ Do you recognise that your soul is resilient once you have traversed the house of Scorpio and entered the 9th house of Sagittarius?
- ❖ How can you focus on moving forward from your past struggles so that you can continue to live in the light?
- ❖ Where in your life is it time to level up and take more responsibility for the things that truly matter?

CHAPTER 34

THE AFTERLIFE DIMENSION

"Through the burning flames of fire, your soul will be seared. Ignited. Purified. Here, left with the remains of wholeness, you will awaken to your most beautiful truth –transformed and reborn."

When our soul is reborn, we must take a moment each day to look into our eyes, for here we will meet our soul's purest blueprint, connecting with the richest light and recognising that we are infinite beings. We must learn to love every part of ourselves without judgement – the shadows and the light – for that is where we shall utilise the power of wholeness.

By the time we have reached the fire of the 9th house, we realise the power in forgiveness. Not only do we have to learn to forgive ourselves for our past pains and limiting beliefs, but we also must learn to forgive others too. If we do not forgive then we will never move forward into the newness of life after loss.

Forgiveness is probably one of the most difficult parts of the journey in evolution. So many of us struggle to forgive others because blame is so prominent in this world, but what we do not realise is that if we cannot ever forgive others then we are unable to forgive ourselves.

The ego can often tangle itself in making up stories about someone's wrongdoing, but this only leaves us trapped in our victimhood. Dancing with the divine in the act of forgiveness opens the door to freedom, which we all deserve. The power of forgiveness can transform people and worlds far greater than we will ever know.

You can create a future that is filled with appreciation, playfulness, relationships, and a career that thrives, financial security, and all-round abundance. The truth is that we all can, and if you are to keep the intention of forgiveness on your path then you will – you will have it all, because the universe operates from a place of love.

Nevertheless, we must be willing to choose love over fear. Always. In any given moment, no matter how hard the challenge is. You must be willing to love yourself and all your humanness. Love the perfection of this world that is imperfect right now. Love how far we have come rather than how far we must go. Love your authentic essence of who you are beneath the surface.

Forgiveness first begins with us. Can you truly forgive yourself for the things, people, and situations that were out of line in the past? What is more, can you truly allow yourself to feel the freedom of this forgiveness when embodied in all your compassion? Doing is one thing. Feeling is another. We can remain trapped in the chambers of our prison for decades, even lifetimes if we have not got it in us to feel forgiveness. If in doubt, feel into forgiveness – it is incredibly powerful.

If you are looking for some answers then look into your eyes. Eyes do not lie. They are the windows to the soul, and they speak only purity. You can spend a few moments looking into a mirror, staring into the depth of your own eyes and know what is happening on this inside. Look closely, for long enough and your soul will begin to tell you all sorts of things. Do not underestimate the power of this amazing exercise – you will be surprised at the instant guidance and clarity you will receive.

Not only does the afterlife dimension teach you to embody forgiveness, but it also opens you up to recognising your immense potential after everything you have overcome. This place beautifully teaches us that we are limitless and that anything is possible. Here is the place where teachers are born to teach lessons of love.

Soul Communication

- ❖ Are you able to invite forgiveness into your life each day?
- ❖ Can you forgive everything and everyone from the bottom of your heart?
- ❖ Do you feel free when you forgive everything and everyone?

CHAPTER 35

THE SOUL'S BLUEPRINT

"Your soul is always guiding you to integrate all the fragmented parts of yourself so that you can live in wholeness."

Stepping into the unique and authentic blueprint of your soul is one of the most profound awakenings you will ever experience. It is the moment we recognise that whatever we wish to manifest in this world, is possible. Stepping into the blueprint of your soul brings forth the greatest version of yourself and speaks of pure alignment. The planet in which we all live on desires for each one of us to be living in alignment with the things that light up the soul, because this is when creativity and intuitive gifts are born into the world. This is when we start learning to be of service to ourselves and others by doing the things we love most – the things that matter most.

When one is mindful about making the effort to raise their vibrations, they can fast learn the difference between being in alignment, vs being completely off track.

Since there is no such thing as permanence and we live in a fast-paced world, it can be extremely easy to move in and out of alignment. We are surrounded by ever-changing ideas and influences. What matters most is that we stay true to ourselves by following the things that light us up each day. We must ensure that we stay focused and fine-tune our energy around that which is positive within our lives, for this is when alignment happens.

I like to class jumping out of bed each morning, beaming with excitement for the day ahead, as being in total alignment with the blueprint of your soul. Snoozing your alarm with no motivation to begin the day, complaining about work before you even get out of the door because you hate the job you do is not alignment.

The simple factor of what makes you feel good is the best way to recognise when your soul and the universe are participating in a harmonious ritual of co-creation.

You can achieve an everyday state of alignment when you relate to your billion-dollar inner guide. From the food you eat to the people you hang out with. In any given moment, we can check-in and know where we stand by simply asking, "How does this make me feel?" And in this case, always trust your body and its messages – intuition never lies.

As one moves through life with a higher state of awareness, they too can bring around extremely powerful energy shifts in all areas of life – health, relationships, career, and lifestyle. Dance with the rhythms of what makes you feel good, and you will be free to navigate your way to the core of your inner magic.

Alignment is when your inner-world becomes a vibrational match to your outer-world. The mastery of integrating mind, body, and soul is the pivotal point of accessing the power to create your reality. If we are powerful enough to change what we feel on the inside, then we are powerful enough to change what we see, live, and breathe on the outside. What we feel, we attract and therefore we must check in with our emotions each day, feeling into everything and simply letting go. When we hold on out of fear, we become stuck, unable to freely move forward. When we become stuck, we stop our alignment with the blueprint of our soul.

Soul Communication

- ❖ When and how are you in alignment with the blueprint of your soul?
- ❖ What might you need to release so that you can become more aligned?
- ❖ What do you need to maintain so that you can stay in flow with the universe?

When we permit the soul to do its work, we move into our unique rhythm. We dance to the beat of our drum, moving with the ever-flowing change of the universe. We allow our soul to guide us to our gold through an effortless journey of positive manifestation.

Being able to reach into the core and no longer need to search for meaning outside oneself is the moment the soul is reborn. Through meditation, creative play, art, writing, adventures, exploring nature, body therapy, and mindfulness, there is a strong sense of exceptional alignment found within the heart of simply being you. Sometimes, we do not need to do everything to have an outcome. By simply doing something with non-attachment, we are surrendering to the rhythms of energy and learning to flow.

Alignment can show up in many beautiful ways, confirming that the universe is in partnership with your mind, body, and soul. For the soul to be an expression of its uniqueness and beauty, there must be a drive or some form of curiosity for tapping into the secret language of the universe and remaining open to all that is. This is often through symbols, numbers, music, colour, and emotion. Poets, artists, designers, writers, and filmmakers tend to be the ones who are deeply connected to the alignment of the universe and soul. These are the people connected to the imagery within the psyche – and metaphorically speaking – these are the ones who can reach the depths of genius and creation through a strong connection to the emotion. Their work is created through manifesting spirit into matter through the flow and rhythms of emotion.

The butterfly is symbolic of transformation – often, the butterfly turns up in your outer world to remind you of your strength during such transition from old to new. Next time you see a butterfly, ask your higher self how you feel at that exact moment. The chances are the butterfly will turn up during your most difficult soul evolving challenges. When you see the butterfly, smile! This is the universe speaking to your heart, and the smallest moment of gratitude will create more magical moments like this.

While I would love to touch on numerology too, this is an extraordinarily lengthy topic, so perhaps I will delve into this another time – perhaps another book. In the meantime, you might feel called to check out your planetary alignments and access your birth chart numerology? If so, please be sure to reach out to my beautiful friend who offers such incredible birth chart readings. Her work brings the elements of art and astrology together in one seamless journey, delivering a unique reading for every single soul. Instagram: @theastroartist

CHAPTER 36

THE 9ᵀᴴ SOUL COMMUNICATION

"When you follow what lights you up, you say yes to being united with your soul."

Find a quiet place where you will not be disturbed, preferably outside in nature, minus the shoes. Sit down and place your hands comfortably on your thighs, palms facing upwards. Close your eyes. Take in a deep breath and hold it there for a few seconds – exhale.

Continue the focus on your breath, deeply breathing in and out as you calm your mind. Repeat the following affirmation three times: *"I choose to connect with my soul."*

Now, remain here in your own heart space and stillness for as long as needed. Focusing on your inner compass, allow the energy to flow up through you from the ground below. As you reach your meditative state of being (since there is no specific way) allow the chaos of thoughts to flow in and out of your mind. Do not assess or stop to judge – just let it all flow.

Spend the next few moments reconnecting to the energy of Mother Nature and her unconditional love. When you have spent enough time here, now move your awareness up to your crown chakra. Open your energy field up to receiving source energy from the Universal Father. Allow the light above to channel down through you. Let this love cleanse your entire mind, body and soul.

Sit here in this space for as long as required. Reach into the depths of your inner being communicating with all its wisdom and clarity. Enjoy the peace within the stillness. Enjoy the inner compass of reaching your light.

How will you know when you are reconnected with your soul? You will feel so centred in the power of love and truth that nobody could pull you away from this space.

Allow this healing energy to flow through you – take the guidance you receive and leave the rest. It never has to be a complicated task – everything is simple when it comes to the soul.

Write a list of the creative things that you would happily do if you had all the money, time, resources, and inspiration in the world.

_____

_____

_____

_____

_____

_____

_____

_____

_____

What activities keep you grounded in the present moment? This can be anything from getting creative with art or taking the dog for a walk on the beach.

_____

_____

_____

_____

_____

_____

_____

_____

_____

_____

List ten people who reinforce a state of presence when in their company and why?

_____

_____

_____

_____

_____

_____

_____

_____

_____

_____

Olivia Blakey

What past experiences in your life might you need to release?

_____

_____

_____

_____

_____

_____

_____

_____

_____

List ten changes you can make so that you can move closer into alignment with your highest good and walk the path of least resistance.

_____

_____

_____

_____

_____

_____

_____

_____

_____

_____

List ten ideas of what 'living in the now' means to you and how these positive moments make you feel.

_____

_____

_____

_____

_____

_____

_____

_____

_____

_____

CHAPTER 37

THE GOAT

"I utilise the power of my mind, body and soul
to create my most authentic life."

Sign: Capricorn
Ruler: Saturn
Element: Earth
Season: Winter
Colour: Brown
Stone: Amber
Light elements: Inspired, Methodical, Wise, Ambitious, Consistent
Shadow elements: Incapable, Helpless, Vulnerable, Lazy, Un-resourceful

When we transform into the 10th house of Capricorn, we are asked to put a focus on all-things career-related – this is where the soul steps into its fully embodied mission. Our career is our soul's blueprint and so much more; it is our gateway to living our most authentic life by doing the work that matters to us most in the world.

The light elements of the Goat speak of inspiration, method, wisdom, ambition, and consistency. It is the pioneering part of the soul that journeys through the most difficult times and always comes out stronger on the other side.

When we journey through this house, we recognise that we are resilient souls that can overcome anything. We understand that because we have made it this far, we can move mountains.

Symbolic of the masculine dimension and the work that we do in the world, we must ask ourselves if our career wellness is thriving. Since we spend much of our time working, we must do work that serves a purpose in making the planet a better place to live. We must be fulfilled by our career, learning new skills and knowledge each day. When we are showing up to learning new ways, we can achieve a sense of fulfilment. The goat represents two parts of the seven dimensions of wellness. This includes career and intellectual wellness.

The career dimension is born from satisfaction and enrichment in work. When you receive fulfilment from your career, you are in a state of occupational wellness. Your career wellness grows when you feel like you are contributing to a positive cause. When you utilise your skills, you attain a sense of achievement.

Here are some tools to align with the career dimension:

- Create a vision board for your goals
- Choose a career that you will enjoy
- Learn new skills
- Study to become a master within your field
- Contribute to creating a better world to live in

The intellectual dimension is born from creativity and expanding knowledge. Intellectual wellness requires spending time upgrading the mind through mental activity. A steady rhythm of mental exercise is vital for mental health.

To be a problem solver and find solutions is to be in a state of intellectual health. When we can find solutions to our problems, we can also make healthy choices for other areas of life.

Here are some tools to align with the intellectual dimension:

- Learn a new language
- Take part in a new course
- Be comfortable with taking on new challenges
- Read more books
- Write in a journal
- Create art

CHAPTER 38

THE MASCULINE DIMENSION

*"I choose to embody the positive elements
of divine masculine nature."*

Without the light elements of the masculine dimension, the feminine dimension is simply unprotected. The masculine dimension brings about qualities that enable the feminine to be in flow with her intuitive and creative rhythms. Positive attributes of the masculine dimension include:

- Assertive
- Courageous
- Independent
- Protective
- Passionate
- Confident
- Decisive
- Open
- Balanced
- Connected

When someone is stuck in the shadows of the masculine, they are completely disconnected from the feminine dimension. This can mean that they feel suppressed and lack creative flow towards life and all its greatness. The negative elements of the masculine dimension are:

- Aggressive
- Competitive
- Co-dependent

- Immature
- Manipulative
- Withdrawn
- Overly protective
- Indecisive
- Imbalanced
- Closed off

We have reached a time in history when trying to make it alone in a masculine world is no longer serving us. We are coming to discover that we need more self-love and healing, not outer circumstances that mask our emotions. We are discovering that somewhere inside of our physical being is a multidimensional aspect which requires great understanding. We may not know what that is – some refer to it as soul, others call it spirit, the universe, God or source. However, what we do know is that if we continue forcing from a place of resistance, we are only going to get more lost in the abyss of our sickness.

When I look back to the days in which I was trapped in my shadow masculine energy, I feel a wave of anxiety ripple through me. That anxiety does not stay with me because I accept its presence now more than ever. It has been my greatest teacher in guiding me to live more harmoniously when it comes to my work life and career. I have found a beautiful balance between doing and being.

I have released the layers upon layers of conditioning that I had created in my mind about believing that I must always be doing rather than simply being. This type of conditioning is no surprise – it is quite possibly one of the worst types of suppression today. If we continue to give our power away to masculine energy and disempower the feminine, humanity could end up stuck on a road to nowhere. I thank my soul each day for prompting me to face my fears of breaking free from the controlling shadows of the masculine energy.

From the 'work hard play harder' programming I'd become fixated on, to the return of my innocence, love and simplicity that I had once embodied as a child, I sit here in deep reverence for the lessons in which the masculine model of society taught me.

The individuation of the soul wants to be expressed in all its illumination, in a balance between the feminine and masculine dimension. We all look at the masculine energy of the sun each day, expressing gratitude for its fierce energy that fuels each moment on earth. But how often do we take the time to honour the moon in all her ever-changing phases? Are we profoundly grateful for these moments of illumination moving through the night, bringing light to the darkness? Or are we denying the feminine energy with sole focus on the masculine?

In a world so driven by action and very little time to simply be, rather than do, it has come to my attention that perhaps we are on our way to breaking point – burnout – because of our disconnect from the soul that is not in harmonious balance between masculine and feminine. Scrap that. We have already reached the breaking point, but thankfully, this is the catalyst for the rebirth of the collective soul of humanity.

You see, like a bird cannot fly with one wing, the masculine cannot endure this work alone. He is, rather, asking for a glimpse of nurture, support, and a sense of unity. Rather than always attempting to make it alone, the masculine is in deep need of having permission to surrender to the soft and receptive, the flow of feminine energy. She permits him to do so. Rather than trying to make it alone, the masculine can hand over the reins to the dark moon of the night – the divine feminine.

Soul Communication

- ❖ What areas of the masculine's light do you need to embody?
- ❖ Where in your life do you need to transcend the masculine shadows?
- ❖ Are you more attracted to the sun or the moon?
- ❖ How are you in balance between your masculine and feminine energy?

Perhaps our lack of connection to the night's moonlight is merely a reflection of the dampened parts of the collective soul. Perhaps in the act of communicating with the soul, we can return to our internal sun and moon; become whole in both aspects.

When we explore the world of polarity, we can learn a little more about ourselves and the universe. Quite simply, polarities are the complementary qualities of the same thing. It is important to know that one polarity will always create its other. Left creates right, up creates down and here creates there.

Understanding our polarities is the key to all wisdom. Finding that balance between the two is the moment we can say goodbye to struggle and resistance; we can be in flow, centred between both ends of the spectrum. For example, when there is a balance between body and mind there is harmony within the soul.

Since each of us owns both masculine and feminine traits, it is fair to assume our inner masculine cannot happen without our feminine and our inner feminine cannot happen without our masculine. The next time you are called to slow down but instead choose to keep pushing and striving, then check in with your soul to find out *why* it is time to slow down. In allowing the steady, receptive, and nourishing energy of your inner feminine to emerge, you will come to learn the power of rest and stillness in the cocoon.

How are you to know when you have perhaps tipped the scales too far to one side?

This is where the body comes into focus. The body is a vessel that delivers emotions which are always attempting to communicate with you. In allowing these signals, messages and impulses to come through, you can hop back onto the centre of your scales and rebalance your energy. Whether it is an uplifting run around the park or a day relaxing in the spa, be sure to listen to what your body, mind, and soul need for the return to spiritual equilibrium.

CHAPTER 39

WORK AND CAREER

"Sometimes, we have to lose everything before we can gain anything."

I believe that it is not our duty to 'save' the planet, but rather, we must save ourselves. For if we can all take the necessary steps to have the love, compassion and nurture that our body, mind and soul need right now, then the planet – our home – will not need saving.

My early twenties were fuelled by such an idea that if I didn't have big names and big ass titles on my CV, then I'd sure as hell be left out in the cold with no successful future ahead of me.

There are millions of people out there with an accumulation of materialism, and yet they are riddled with stress, anxiety, and everything else that comes with the feeling of never having enough. There are millions of people out there who have bank balances that enable them to drink forty thousand-dollar bottles of champagne, and yet they have never felt so lonely and disconnected from their true nature.

We have reached a time in history that reflects the once hidden truth that making it in a masculine world is no longer serving us. We are coming to discover that we need more love, not things. We are finding out that we need more health, not work overload. We are finding out that somewhere inside of our physical being is a multidimensional aspect which requires great understanding.

Soul Communication

❖ What areas of your life is your soul asking you to step inwards to so that you can do the inner work?

❖ If you have done the inner work, then what areas of your life is your soul asking you to step up?

❖ If you have done the inner work and already stepped up, then what areas of your life is your soul asking you to step out of?

I invite you to take a few moments to simply 'be'. Simply be in the beauty of all that you already are. The beginning of all transcendence is activated when one can witness their magnitude right here, right now without any need to analyse. We must always be dedicated to shifting out of mind and into the heart – the most profound way to do this is through play.

If you do not take some time to look in the mirror each day and remind yourself how amazing you are, then start now. In the conscious effort to remember how powerful we indeed are, we create a ripple effect on the entire universe! We motivate, heal, inspire, and elevate ourselves and everyone else on the planet. Be the change you want to see in the world.

In the sheer moment of finding just the smallest glimpse of courage to let go and grow, we say yes to all that is available waiting on the other side.

While it seems easier to avoid and resist the challenges that come our way, the truth can only be found when you choose to walk through the burning flames. These fiery flames are here to leave you with the remains; the purest element of all – ash. And only when you have destroyed what you are not, will you find what you are.

Waking up from the illusion of what you once thought and believed to be true, is not the easiest process. You feel cheated about life, questioning everything – your sanity, future, career, relationships, your entire existence – but it is a moment that allows you to make sense of the struggles and suffering of the past.

It is significant to not get stuck in the stage of questioning everything, because staying stuck in this stops you from learning the newness that is trying to come through. This newness is the language of the soul.

The greatest action any human can take is surrender. Surrendering yourself to the crumbling of all things that no longer serve you. When you surrender, you crack open and that is where light enters, penetrating every part of your being. When the light enters, the gates to liberation and freedom open.

Being an empath in a stifled society is the greatest challenge that the collective soul of humanity currently faces. We have been born into a world that values thinking over feeling, that has done so for centuries, leaving us caught up in an imbalance between masculine and feminine polarities.

Being an empath can be a gift as well as a curse. Such emotional intelligence enables someone to be one of the greatest communicators on the planet, yet the overwhelming depths of feeling everything in a suppressed society often leads to participating in the worst forms of escapism.

For as long as we value thinking over feeling, humanity will unconsciously seek ways to remain numb, avoiding the 'negative' at all costs.

Ten years of denying, resisting, and suppressing and bottling up these wounds led to being hospitalised after a near-death experience in 2018.

Pain is not an entity that must be banished. If we are to allow our pain to speak to us, without attempting to suppress the message that is trying to emerge, then pain can be one of our greatest teachers in life. It teaches us our birth-right and that is love. Allowing pain into your life does not therefore mean that this becomes your identity either.

I want to highlight this part because I was so coiled up in the dramas of everything that had previously happened to me, that suddenly my attachment to this painful story, somehow anchored so deep into my roots that I could only be associated with this version of reality. If we are to associate the entire story around pain, then we are playing out the victim role. However, when we are feeling challenged by rebirth, attachment to past pains and experiences is not the solution.

It is no falsehood to accept that humanity is living in a time where the darkest elements of our nature have been suppressed through societal conditioning. We have become preoccupied about what we believe happiness should be, attempting to strive for perfection, when we are already perfect. Happiness is simple – we do not have to complicate things. The soul's mission is simple too – it speaks one language that is unconditional love.

It is no surprise that like many other humans on this planet, I was afraid to show the parts of me that were associated with darkness, and so I moulded into a society through the unconscious act of numbing with all sorts of band-aids, masking what was really happening below the surface.

It was only when I embarked on a journey of meditation in which I began to meet the fragmented parts of myself, showing me all sorts of chaos that lived within. I came to discover that everything that had unfolded in my outer world was a direct reflection of my inner compass and how my thoughts had emitted a certain frequency that the universe simply brought back to me.

My mind, and the thoughts that spiralled through my entire being had embodied that which only knew fear and pain. I had become trapped in my own prison, and each time I attempted to get above the surface, in a power struggle of resisting my truth, I would be dragged back down into dark waters.

The more I pushed away the fears, the more they were highlighted. The more they became highlighted, the more I felt the need to reach outside of myself to stop the noise. It was only during my moments of total surrender the following year that I discovered that keeping things simple is the ultimate solution.

CHAPTER 40

THE 10TH SOUL COMMUNICATION

*"When you finally face your deepest fears you
will, in fact, uncover your greatest gifts."*

Most of our fears stem from the patriarchal society in which we have been living in. It is important to get to the root of our fears so that we can pour more love into the masculine dimension. Since we have now journeyed through the feminine and masculine elements, let us unite these two dimensions with unconditional love so that fear can be transcended to light. It is the role of the divine feminine to nurture, nourish and heal the divine masculine's fearful ways of thinking.

Tap into your heart and all that you have learned so far so that you can discover what is holding you back. Consciously choose to finally transcend this. Feel into your emotions and align with your brightest of light.

My biggest fears are:

_____

_____

_____

_____

_____

_____

_____

_____

_____

_____

The things that trigger my fears are:

_____

_____

_____

_____

_____

_____

_____

_____

_____

_____

When I let my fears overpower me it leaves me feeling:

_____

_____

_____

_____

_____

_____

_____

_____

_____

In embracing my fears, I will perhaps discover that:

_____

_____

_____

_____

_____

_____

_____

_____

_____

_____

My fear is teaching me to:

_____

_____

_____

_____

_____

_____

_____

_____

_____

_____

Through embracing my fears, I will be able to do the following:

_____

_____

_____

_____

_____

_____

_____

_____

The positivity and gift that comes from transcending my fears is:

_____

_____

_____

_____

_____

_____

_____

_____

_____

_____

I trust that my fears are calling me to overcome them so that I can achieve the following:

_____

_____

_____

_____

_____

_____

_____

_____

_____

CHAPTER 41

THE WATER BEARER

"I know that I am the master of my soul's mission."

Sign: Aquarius
Ruler: Uranus
Element: Air
Season: Winter
Colour: Turquoise
Stone: Amethyst
Light elements: Individualistic, Humanitarian, Inventive, Original, Calm
Shadow elements: Judgemental, Opinionated, Detached, Disconnected, Careless

When we step into the house of Aquarius, we are being called to see through the eyes of subjectivity. We are being asked to remember that every single one of us on the planet is experiencing a different reality and this requires the purest of empathy.

This is a place where we can finally see through different lenses carrying forward all the wisdom we have gathered. This is a place where we can step out into the world after we have been through the process of rebirth, sharing our wisdom by helping others.

Aquarius is where our soul's light shines bright as we embody pure individualism. We recognise that all our experiences in the world are subjective and that is what enables us to do humanitarian work in the world. Other light elements include inventiveness, originality and calmness. When we journey here, we can focus on being the art director of manifesting all our dreams.

Those who are stuck in the shadows of Aquarius are often judgemental, overly opinionated, detached from reality, disconnected from their truth, and live carelessly.

If we are to be the best version of ourselves then this is certainly a place where we will learn that. By the time we have reached this house, we have gathered so much wisdom which should be liberating. We have been through the process of rebirth and everything we have discovered becomes the catalyst for surrender.

Symbolic of seeing through different lenses, I would like to make emphasis on this being the place where our inner medicine man/woman is born. By now, we have learned the balance between masculine and feminine nature and embodying this into all areas of our life. Aquarians are usually the ones who focus on humanitarian projects, delivering great causes that are connected to the needs of the community. They often work with animals, protecting their welfare on the planet.

If anything, here we learn that humanity is far stronger when united. We learn that every action in the world creates a butterfly effect and that is why we must be conscious about the choices that we make.

CHAPTER 42

THE SUBJECTIVE DIMENSION

"Western society calls it mental illness. Ancient shamanic traditions call it spiritual emergence. I call it rebirth."

We are one collective soul experiencing subjective encounters – we all see through different lenses.

In 2018 I went through a traumatic experience following the depression. When I ended up in hospital, I had an out of body experience (OBE) where I was looking down over my body and could see the doctors and nurses surrounding me.

I was pure consciousness in complete divine light, and everything below looked like darkness. I went through some sort of life review. It felt like my soul was teaching me that separation is an illusion and there is only unconditional love in this world. When I woke up anchored back in my body, I knew my life would never be the same again. We are divine light beings. This was my experience of discovering the pure connection to the soul and all its unconditional love and light. While this was my experience, others may share this insight with their own experiences, and others may not.

Extreme resistance to what we are unwilling to change is what causes suffering and often leads to mental breakdown or illness. In the year 2018, my reality cracked open so wide that I was hospitalised and diagnosed with psychosis after 5 days of sleep deprivation. I had completely disconnected from my reality.

The western medicine model defines mental illness as, 'A condition which causes serious disorder in a person's behaviour or thinking.' Let us look at this through a different lens. Amazonian shamanic traditions define mental illness as, 'Spiritual emergencies and crisis that birth a healer.'

I have received support from both models of medicine. I must state that both models have supported me in many ways, but now I am content with simply being myself without the need to medicate. For me, equine therapy has and always will be my greatest medicine. I owe my life to horses, for they have guided me out of turmoil and into a state of presence.

I was diagnosed with psychosis but from here onwards, I will refer to it as a spiritual emergency. I had just turned twenty-six and my reality had completely cracked open, shattered into a thousand pieces. Fragile and vulnerable, I craved a connection to the heart space that equine therapy brings. Something that was non-judgemental, simple, peaceful and unconditional.

My ego had been put through a psychological death and these animals somehow helped me to recover from the suffering that had consumed me for over a decade. They helped remind me that I must get up and show up to live life joyfully, instead of staying stuck in a dark hole of nothingness. They told me that I needed a purpose. I felt like a blank slate, perplexed, and confused; unsure where to start over.

Cleaning out stables reminded me of the importance of keeping a clean house. Feeding them, prompting me of the importance of healthy eating to stay anchored in my body – grounded. Riding horses teaches the importance of exercise and movement to shift stagnant energy and feel revitalized. It is a sport that liberates your soul as you enter your true state of being here in the now, totally focused on the task, balanced between mind and body.

Was it a coincidence that the job I landed required taking care of seven horses – one which was called 'Spirit', at the time I was overcoming the impacts of a spiritual emergency? I think not. Somehow, this gave me the hope, faith, and trust that I was being protected through my rebirthing process. When so many of us are going through the struggles of rebirthing the soul it can be hard to show up to work commitments, but these horses somehow saved me. I was paid to take care of them and in return, they took care of me. I had opened the door to communication of the soul, and I had to learn this new language. This new language was about surrendering to the truth that the universe always wants to support us and will always have our back.

When I was a teenager, I learned the power of discipline and how this was required to care for these animals. This discipline has positively programmed me to get up and show up in all areas of my life. Showing up to different equestrian competitions and really diving into the work of equestrian training and being in harmony with nature and its energy, was no different to what is required for soulful evolution of humanity.

I was taught the need for showing up to the importance of doing the mundane parts of the job, like mucking out stables, as well as enjoying the exhilaration of riding. It is a process when working with horses; people think you are just sat in the saddle all day but there is far more to it and that is what makes you a disciplined soul.

Transcending fear to love requires digging deep into the psyche to do some sort of gardening ritual. Gardening and removing the weeds of fear, so that we can embrace the beauty and plant seeds of love. Being connected to horses allowed me to travel and experience many different countries. I spent five polo seasons in various states of Australia – wherever I was with horses, I was home. I owe my life to these beautiful beings – we are so blessed to share this earth with the animal kingdom.

Children and horses are the gatekeepers between spirit and matter – they reflect the purest elements of an untainted soul, guided by communication of the heart – feeling rather than thinking.

As humans age, we gather pain that is often projected onto us by others, or even worst, inflicted upon ourselves. Collecting garbage from adolescent experiences, and holding onto this, we transition into adulthood, wondering why life seems so dull and difficult. We mask the pain and attempt to overcome such dullness by numbing ourselves, which often lead to addictions. Our addictions are not the cause of the problem – they are the symptoms and often they are the absence of connection to divine feminine nature. We must seek within to get to the root of the problem and lovingly work on transcending this. We must reconnect to our feminine nature which unconditionally loves and nurtures.

The ego has been built to believe that reaching out for help and surrendering goes against the idea about what is required to be a successful person. But what do we define as success? For most who live in the rat race of western society, success is seen as getting out of bed, turning up to work and pushing through the day.

Soul Communication

❖ What does abundance mean for you?

❖ What are you doing each day to become aligned with your abundance?

I would say that one thing I have discovered through trying to make it in such a fast-paced society is that without my health, I am nothing. So, taking time off work or reaching out for support when we are most in need of understanding our deepest inner turmoil is perhaps the most powerful decision one can make. For when we tune into our inner compass and allow the ego mind to rest, we can begin to discover that perhaps our most profound inner turmoil is serving to be the catalyst for transformation. Perhaps it is forcing us to slow down, reflect and make a new transition on our path.

I write this book to share my findings, so you too can discover the high power within, understanding that we do not have to be separate from the heart space, but rather, we can embody this nourishing life-giving force to empower the lives of ourselves and others. We can create experiences that are of higher consciousness which are embodied in health being our greatest wealth. It is not that you are separate from love – you are the gateway to love.

Soul Communication

❖ How do you consciously shift out of mind and into the heart?

❖ What do you do each day to enter your heart space?

The conscious elements of the masculine dimension offer discipline, freedom, passion, action, and individuation. The unconscious elements play out in the world as fear, greed, distrust and separation.

If we are to make the mindful effort to breakthrough unconscious programming and release old ways of living, through lovingly integrating the ego, we can begin to shift into a new way of being that utilises the power of the divine masculine. Therefore, opening space to work in more harmonious flow with the nourishment, creativity and unity consciousness that the feminine is attempting to rebirth right here on this planet.

In Hindu traditions, Shiva is represented as the consciousness in which the great life force – Shakti – lives within. They are united together in harmony. Without Shiva, Shakti simply cannot preside – for, without consciousness, Shakti becomes Kali, who is simply seen as dancing on the empty corpse of Shiva. Without Shakti, Shiva is merely a stagnant body in which the disconnection to the very life force simply creates meaningless around the gift of consciousness and the great things we can do for ourselves, others and the planet.

It is therefore obvious to discover that these elements are two sides of the same coin and therefore one cannot exist without the other. I invite you to tap into your inner masculine dimension and reflect upon the unconscious elements that show up in your life each day, perhaps asking yourself why and how you can release these. I then invite you to tap into your inner masculine dimension and reflect upon the conscious elements that show up in your life each day, giving gratitude to these gifts and further reflecting how you can integrate more of these traits into the aspects of the feminine – for that, is where true power can be born.

The Mayans predicted that the world would end in 2012. To many, this seemed like a totally invalid prediction, but what many did not understand is that it was an ending of the old consciousness. Instead, this ending was happening so that a new paradigm within the collective soul of humanity could be birthed.

If we are to look back over the last decade, so much has changed. We have walked through a door into a world that has created new forms of technology and communication, as well as understanding that the rapid increase of mental health concerns requires our attention.

Such patterns of forcing the body and mind to operate in robotic style overload are crumbling. It is a great time to be alive in this new earth consciousness for we are offered new ways and opportunities to liberate ourselves. We are being given so much choice that enables us to evolve and elevate higher.

When it came to forming the idea of writing this book, I was overwhelmed about the paradoxical theme that seems to run throughout this story. Here I am praising and giving gratitude to the freedom in which technology has given us, yet somehow this gift is too a curse, if we are not to use it wisely.

Yes, we have elevated in one respect. Still, to dive into this new existence full force, with little room to simply 'be' a human being who is at one with nature then we are no different to the masculine dimension in which we have long been stuck in trying to attain more and more. Money and success? I would say not. I would say that being able to work independently is more potent than ever. I say this because, in 2017, I had come to discover that I was living in my own freedom, working freelance as a digital marketing consultant. But on the inside, I was destroyed.

My career looked dazzling. I lived in a high rise two-bedroom apartment with a swimming pool and had a wardrobe full of colour. I had everything that city life had to offer and would often attend wild parties with friends on the weekend. It all seemed fun on the outside, posting my every move on social media, attempting to somehow convince myself that 'this' was the life.

I could not have been more wrong if I had tried. The funniest part in all of this is that there were several times in which I said, *"Screw it"* and packed up my belongings to go work polo seasons across Australia.

So many would say to me, *"But you're on a great salary"*, or *"Do you think you'll regret it?"* Others would cheer me on with support in admiration about the courage and resilience that somehow seemed to drive me towards a more fulfilling life.

The many times in which I took the plunge to serve my soul with the concept of less being more, my ego would often play tricks with me about how I must remain focused on 'making it' in my career. But the universe always has more beautiful and bigger plans for us. It is only through surrender in allowing this great force to move us into joy and abundance that we come to discover that nothing is ever a waste.

We are only surviving when we are anxious about the need to attain more. We are only surviving when we are solely living in the masculine dimension. However, we can begin to thrive when we become in balance between the feminine and masculine nature, honouring slowing down as well as taking action. Sometimes, we do not need to do more and attain more things – we need more love and connection.

Soul Communication

❖ Where in your life do you feel like you are just surviving?
❖ Where in your life do you feel like you are thriving?

CHAPTER 43

YOUR SOUL'S PURPOSE

"Stop pushing, stop forcing, and stop looking outside of yourself.
You are a product of perfection with all the answers inside
of you. This is where you will find your soul's purpose."

All we have is now. In this very moment of bringing our attention to the present, we create an incredibly potent opportunity for expansion, love and abundance.

A state of presence requires one to be centred entirely in their values and anchored in their heart's desires. I have worked with many people who approach their values far too wishy-washy. I was once this person. The truth is that we must know why we are making a change to our lives – if you do not understand why then you will never honestly know where you are going.

Soul Communication

- ❖ How does it feel to be guided by love?
- ❖ What does it mean to you to be driven by your inner guide?
- ❖ How does it make you feel when you are living from an empowered mindset that is programmed by love and abundance?
- ❖ What do you believe to be your purpose in this lifetime?

And just for the record – you are not the teenager who got rejected at school, nor the depression you suffered last year or years before. You are neither the person who was made redundant, ended up in debt, or lost their entire family. You are so much more than that, so focus on the positive aspects of your life.

The universe would like to bring you more joy if that is where you focus your energy. You are a boundless being, abundant in existence, with unlimited potential to create the exact life that you do want and deserve – right here and now. So, take your lessons, your scars, your wounds, and your challenges. Take them and use their wisdom to write your most excellent story yet. Re-write your purpose in alignment with unconditional love.

CHAPTER 44

THE 11ᵀᴴ SOUL COMMUNICATION

"Be the change you want to see in the world."

What areas in your life feel forced, and why do you need to release them?

_____

_____

_____

_____

_____

_____

_____

_____

_____

_____

List the reasons why you continue to do the things that feel forced. It is okay to feel vulnerable – that is the whole point of this task – if in doubt, surrender.

_____

_____

_____

_____

_____

_____

_____

_____

_____

What would you do every single day if you had all the money in the world?

_____

_____

_____

_____

_____

_____

_____

_____

_____

What emotions do you need to tap into to become a vibrational alignment for attaining more of the things you love?

_____

_____

_____

_____

_____

_____

_____

_____

_____

If you could diminish all fear in this very moment and had all the money in the world, what things would you dive right into today?

Write a list of all the things in your life that would completely align with your soul.

_____

_____

_____

_____

_____

_____

_____

_____

Olivia Blakey

Soul Communication

I choose the boundless love that connects sun to moon. I choose joy and wisdom through the painful lessons I have learned. I choose abundance because I deserve no less than a beautiful existence. May all those who are facing their fears or doubts be gently guided to remember the beauty that lives within all experiences. Everything serves a purpose in this universe. So be it!

CHAPTER 45

THE FISH

"I believe that I am a limitless being with boundless potential. My belief systems are surrounded by love"

Sign: Pisces
Ruler: Neptune
Element: Water
Season: Winter
Colour: Ocean Green
Stone: Labradorite
Light elements: Dreamy, Artistic, Humane, Empathic, Sensitive
Shadow elements: Ungrounded, Separated, Irresponsible, Lazy, Isolated, Questioning

When we enter the last and final astrological house, we are being called to put everything into full perspective regarding that which we have learned. We are at the end of the cycle of the soul and this is the place where the magic happens as we surrender to old ways. When we finally surrender to releasing that which no longer serves us, we open up to that which is meant to bring the new by gathering all wisdom we have discovered throughout the astrological journey and putting everything into practice so that we can live our best life.

The fish is symbolic of oneness and unity, where all things come together in divine harmony. The fish teach us that we are living in a dualistic world where here creates there, up creates down, left creates right, and with fear comes love. This place gives us the faith and hope that we can turn all negatives into positives, darkness into light, and transform our fears and demons into creativity, joy, abundance, and unconditional love. The beautiful light elements of Pisces ask us to be free in all that we do – to dive deep into all our mystery and swim the ocean of magic.

Pisces people are born from art, music and all creativity that gives rise to the visionary world that we live in. I am a Pisces sun and rising – I have double the water in my birth chart and while this can appear to be very dreamy energy, it can also be overwhelming at times. These people are anchored deep in their hearts with empathic and intuitive abilities that often create so much sensitivity within their lives. When we are living in a world that is driven by money, power, greed, and times that are shaped around fearful competition, then these Pisceans often feel out of place. We Pisceans need to do everything we can to stay grounded on the earth, anchoring spirit into matter through our peaceful ways of going about life.

Since rebirthing my soul through understanding where I sit within astrology, my life has never been the same. I understand myself better than ever, knowing what serves me and what destroys me. I have found a beautiful balance between my inner and outer worlds, giving, and receiving, doing and being.

I have transformed so much of my darkest shadows into the purest of love and light through writing, being connected with horses, dancing to my favourite music, putting paintbrush to canvas and embracing my own divinity each day with a simple approach to operating in the 5th dimension of spirit.

Most of us feel like the 5th dimension is too complex to understand when it is simpler than ever. It is simple because it is seeing through the eyes of love. Pisces rejoices in endings knowing that there are new beginnings, reminding us that there is always a new cycle of love waiting ahead of us. Pisces reminds us that we are spiritual beings having a beautiful temporary human experience.

When we journey through the last house, we are being called to be the most whole version of ourselves. We are being called to be the greatest creators in manifesting our own magic and anchoring this into the world.

We are being called to tap into oneness and not be afraid of our fears, but rather, transcend them into the deepest of love.

Here, in this last house, we begin to recognise who we really are and strip away everything that we are not. We prepare ourselves for yet another transition back into the house of Aries where we become even stronger leaders of the things that matter in the world. We embody life in all its beauty and magic. We become the art director of our own life, recognising that we are powerful enough to move mountains and that anything is possible.

Before I finish this chapter, I would like to mention my deepest of gratitude for my stepmother who is pretty much a mother to me. She has shown me that I can move mountains and that anything is possible through her support. This woman taught me to move forward and continue shining my light even during the darkest moments. I am deeply grateful for her healing, creative and positive Pisces energy that she reflects to me every single day.

CHAPTER 46

THE SPIRITUAL DIMENSION

"We are waves from the same ocean."

When we operate in the 5th dimension, we are always living with the sincerest intentions that emanate from the heart. When we live in the vibration of our soul's purest identity, we remember that oneness is our birth-right and that we are connected to all living things – near and far.

A spiritual awakening is not always easy to experience in the beginning stages. At first, you feel cheated about life, questioning absolutely everything – your sanity, your future, your career, your relationships, your entire existence. Nevertheless, there is light at the end of the tunnel. Everything always works out perfectly, unfolding in divine order.

It is significantly vital not to get stuck in the stage of questioning everything, because staying trapped in this shadow element stops you from learning the newness that is trying to come through. This newness is, in fact, the language of the soul. The most significant action any human can take is surrender. You are surrendering yourself to the crumbling of all things that no longer serve you. When you quit resisting the newness to come through, you crack open, and that is where light enters, penetrating every part of your being. When the light enters, the gates to liberation and freedom open.

For me, the greatest form of surrender I have discovered is through my connection to horses. They are my gatekeepers. They are my messengers of the soul. They are my kindred spirits. They open my gates to the spiritual dimension because these animals are incredibly wise at teaching humans to simply be. From these beautiful beings, we learn that everything is what it is.

When I feel that I am closed off from spiritual freedom, it is more than likely because I have lacked spending time with horses. As soon as I feel closed off, I take the time out to connect with these animals and suddenly I remember my true nature. I remember why I am here on this earth. They remind me to learn to love my empathic abilities. They remind me that there is magic everywhere and I can tap into it at any given moment. They teach humanity to see through the eyes of love and to know what it truly means to be grounded on the earth.

I was ten years old when I first sat in the saddle. It was the moment I opened the door to my destiny. Some people are just born to ride, naturally connected to the souls of horses. There is something about these majestic beings that imprints you with a sense of 'knowing' transferring the purest of love through their superpowers.

In 2018 my wonderful nephew travelled from the cosmic womb into the earth realm – his arrival taught me that children also have superpowers of love.

When humans are born into the world, they are a blank canvas with no sense of self, emanating light in its purest form. They radiate love because essentially, they are cleansed vessels who are directly channelling light from spirit into matter. Where there is new life, there is an opportunity for renewal in all forms.

When one is completely anchored in the mission of their soul, they are operating as a gatekeeper. Gatekeepers have one foot in the world of spirit and one foot in the world of matter – combining the 5th dimension with the 3rd dimension. These people understand the sacredness of life and see all through the eyes of love. They are their own billion-dollar guides and they know what they want.

When you can witness human existence through a new lens, you have entered the process of spiritual awakening. This is the beginning of a beautiful journey – rebirth.

Your gatekeeper can be anyone or anything – it can be painting, dancing or any form of creating. Your gatekeeper could be your best friend, partner or even your dog. Perhaps you are feeling so aligned with everything in your life, that you feel like your own gatekeeper? It does not matter what or who is your gatekeeper, but rather, you recognise how powerful this connection is and hold the deepest of gratitude for it.

When you have journeyed through all houses, and finally reach the spiritual dimension, you begin to realise that gratitude is what has got you here and it will always be your superpower. Take a moment to breathe in the gratitude for the unconditional love that your gatekeepers bring into your life. Know that when you are fulfilling a balanced dance between spirit and matter, heart and mind, body and soul, you are in total harmony with the universe – your gates to spiritual freedom are open. When you are open, you receive far more magic in your life. More magic than you can comprehend.

Soul Communication

❖ What or who are your gatekeepers?

❖ Are your gates to spiritual freedom closed or open?

❖ How does your gatekeeper act as a bridge between spirit and matter?

We are living in a time where much of humanity are living with their gates closed because of their fears. What a shame, to never truly experience the individuation of the pure soul. We must release anything that holds us back and step into unconditional love being our guidance. We must affirm that we are worthy of receiving everything we need to fully live in our hearts. We all must empower each other to open the gates within our hearts and lead the most healthy, abundant and loving lives.

The aim of this book is to remove these blocks and become the gatekeeper of your own life. If you have completed the previous eleven Soul Communication exercises, then you have one left to go. You will have surrendered to the fears that hold you back, opening space for new and more loving energy. The last Soul Communication is on the way, and this will certainly bring about powerful magic to manifest your goals and dreams.

CHAPTER 47

YOUR SOUL'S MAGIC

"Your soul is where your greatest power lives;
reclaim it, live it, and breathe it."

Often, there are times that one wishes for far more courage within their heart. The courage to pursue things that appear out of reach. Usually, there are times that one prays for far more strength within their bones. The power to move mountains in the weakest of moments. Often, there are times that one asks for far more passion to be in their blood. The desire for completely encompassing all that they are in their authenticity. But the truth is that we are already all of this. You are already courageous. You are already resilient. You are already passionate. You are already the entire universe. And only when one truly steps into their heart (so they can be guided by the callings of their soul), will they finally recognise that they already have it all. Go within, and there you will find your inner truth.

The magic of your soul is always waiting for you to tap into it. The magic of your soul can be mirrored in all areas of your life – the work you do, the family you have, the soul tribe in your life, the way you treat yourself and the planet.

Your soul is equipped with the wisdom and knowledge of truly embodying your magic and the chances are that the things you do well are the things that are always meant to be for you. There is no need to fear the things you love and desire in your life not coming to you – it is already yours and will soon be on its way to you. All you must do is believe in the magic of your soul and become the master of your magic. Embody it. Practice it. Love it. Nurture it and cherish it.

May your soul softly speak to you through the echoes of the universe, dear one. It is time to step into your most significant potential because all that you desire is ready to be claimed in the centre of your soul. You have done the work, now it is time to believe in the magic of rebirth and move forward with boundless potential. Let us journey through the last Soul Communication.

Once you have completed this then know that you have clearly and intentionally done your very best to release old programming. You have done your very best to become aligned with the love, joy, and abundance that you completely deserve. The next part of the process is to trust in the beauty of the universe that hears your dreams.

It is so essential to hold the vision in your heart each day of what you would like to create. It is said that energy flows where attention goes. Know that the cosmos is supporting all your dreams and you have embarked on the journey of soulful rebirth. It is the laws of the universe to respond.

CHAPTER 48

THE 12ᵀᴴ SOUL COMMUNICATION

"Remember when you wanted what you currently have? Be grateful for what you have while manifesting what you want."

The universe responds positively to gratitude, bringing you more of what you love. Write a list of ten things/people/experiences you are deeply grateful for.

Ten things, I am grateful for:

_____

_____

Olivia Blakey

_____

_____

_____

_____

_____

_____

_____

Ten people, I am grateful for:

_____

_____

_____

_____

_____

_____

_____

_____

_____

Ten experiences, I am grateful for:

_____

_____

_____

_____

_____

_____

_____

_____

_____

_____

Soul Communication

Across time and space, I choose now to allow my fear to come through. I sit in this uncomfortable space, allowing all that I need to hear come through my soul's voice. I let all that I need to see, journey through my visions. I allow all that I need to know, to be known, and allow all that I need to feel, journey through my emotions. May all beings be supported in transcending fear to faith. So be it!

To transform our lives through the language of the soul, we must also be willing to allow ourselves to feel good. We must align with joy. If we want abundance in our lives, then we must visualise and feel that abundance, as if it is happening right now. Writing a letter from your soul allows you to get into a feel-good place. The power of positive feelings, combined with strong words, can only create more of this energy. It is the law of the universe to respond to such high vibes.

Write a letter to yourself, from your soul. Imagine yourself a year from now – this is called scripting. Scripting is a great tool for manifesting your dreams into reality by visualising your future self. It anchors everything that you would like to attain into the present moment. It helps you to achieve your goals because you are putting pen to paper – anchoring spirit into matter. When we write things down, we give so much more power towards eliminating the old and opening to receive the new.

Soul Communication

* ❖ How are you feeling?
* ❖ Where are you living?
* ❖ What are you doing for work?

213

- ❖ What do your finances look like?
- ❖ Who are you connected to on a soul level?
- ❖ Who are you connected to on a physical level?
- ❖ What does your health and state of mind reflect at this current moment?

Take note of all the things that light you up and send this message out to the universe. You can and will create the life you want through visualising and writing the person you desire to be and the things you would like to change/attract/feel to become more aligned. Manifestation knocks on the door of a disciplined and focused mindset, a heart that believes in the power of the universe and a soul that is open to receiving love and magic.

If you would like to produce an even more reliable connection between your soul and the universe, then be sure to read your letter out loud each morning to start your day with the purest of intentions. You will become more aligned with your highest vibrational frequency. Speaking dreams into existence.

Now write your letter and hold the vision in your heart. Once you have completed this, you have fulfilled the twelve soul communications.

Honour the work you have done in this book and all that you have learned, for you have chosen to become more aligned with your highest vibration of love by dedicating your time and energy to these tasks.

You can go back to this work at any time you wish to re-shape your soul's journey since rebirth is an ever-evolving process.

Printed in the United States
by Baker & Taylor Publisher Services